On Soviet D...

ROY MEDVEDEV

ON SOVIET DISSENT

INTERVIEWS WITH PIERO OSTELLINO

Translated from the Italian by William A. Packer
Edited by George Saunders

Columbia University Press   New York

In 1977 Roy Medvedev completed a series of interviews with Piero Ostellino,
then Moscow correspondent for Corrière della Séra,
on dissent in the Soviet Union;
these interviews were published in Italian as Intervista sul dissenso in URSS.
On Soviet Dissent is a translation of Intervista,
with an additional chapter by Roy Medvedev, "Dissent in the USSR, 1978–79: Failures and
Hopes."
William A. Packer translated the Italian text;
George Saunders translated the Preface to the Paperback Edition
and chapter 10 from the Russian and annotated
and edited the entire text. "Dissent in the USSR, 1980,"
an edited translation of Vittorio Zucconi's interview with Roy Medvedev,
"Ma un nuovo dissenso sta nascendo"
(published on February 4, 1980,
in Corrière della Séra), is printed by permission of the publisher.

Library of Congress Cataloging in Publication Data

Medvedev, Roĭ Aleksandrovich.
On Soviet dissent.

Translation of Intervista sul dissenso in URSS.
Includes bibliographical references and index.
1. Russia—Politics and government—1953–
2. Dissenters—Russia. 3. Medvedev, Roĭ Aleksandrovich. I. Ostellino, Piero. II. Saunders, George,
1936–   III. Title.
DK274.M3513   323.1'47   79-27877
ISBN 0-231-04812-2
ISBN 0-231-04813-0   (pa)

Columbia University Press
New York   Guildford, Surrey

Copyright © 1980, 1985 Columbia University Press
Intervista sul dissenso in URSS © Giuseppe Laterza & Figli
Roma-Bari 1977

Contents

Preface to the Paperback Edition

The Dissident Movement, 1981–1984

Note: This preface was written shortly before the death of Konstantin Chernenko and his immediate replacement as general secretary on March 11, 1985, by Mikhail Gorbachev, a former secretary of the Central Committee and member of the Politburo, as well as a confidant of the late Yuri Andropov. Those events do not alter the relevance of the preface, however, as regards the state of the Soviet dissident movement from 1981 through 1984. It remains to be seen whether the coming of a younger generation of leaders to the helm in the person of the 54-year-old Gorbachev will make a significant difference for the human rights movement in the USSR or for greater democracy in Soviet society in General.

Zhores Medvedev

Preface to the Paperback Edition

The Dissident Movement, 1981–1984

The dissident movement had its greatest impact on intellectual life in the USSR between 1967 and 1977. During that time, despite the differing points of view of its various component groups, the movement as a whole created an alternative ideology and competed rather successfully with the mighty propaganda apparatus of the state. This situation served as the basis for many studies written outside the USSR and was the background to my interviews of 1977 with Piero Ostellino, which form the bulk of the present book. Although the democratic-minded opposition was able to compete successfully with the propaganda apparatus, it could not of course stand up against the repression that intensified so sharply in 1977 and after. Elsewhere I have discussed the reasons for this change in the movement's fortunes, pointing out in particular that it was related to the orientation adopted by many of the dissident groups, namely, not to rely on liberal groups or potential opposition groups within the USSR but to place the main hope on support from outside the country, above all from the United States, since the Carter administration was extending direct and vocal support to the Soviet human rights movement.

In this Preface I wish to discuss the effects that the changes in the top Soviet leadership have had on the dissident movement. This period of change and transition really began in early 1982 with the death of Mikhail Suslov and his replacement as top party ideologist by Yuri Andropov, formerly head of the KGB, although the most obvious change came with the death of Leonid Brezhnev and Andropov's assumption of the post of general secretary in November 1982. After Andropov also died (in early 1984) the period of transition continued. Chernenko was merely a transitional figure. He was old and infirm and had limited political influence. Despite the weakening of the top party and government leadership associated with these changes, repression against political oppositionists did not diminish but intensified.

The period 1981–84 has unfortunately been a time of many serious losses for the opposition movement. Repression increased as early as the beginning of 1980 with the invasion of Afghanistan and the removal of Academician Andrei Sakharov from Moscow to enforced residence in the city of Gorky, and it continued through 1981 and 1982. The authorities had clearly set themselves the task of eliminating all manifestations of organized opposition, including groups with as few as ten or fifteen members. In fact all legal, religious, and national opposition groups were broken up, along with groups advocating women's rights, the rights of handicapped persons, and some small organizations of blue-collar and white-collar workers, such as the SMOT (see footnote in text, p. 7).

The dramatic events in Poland in 1980–81, unlike the Prague Spring of 1968 in Czechoslovakia, which had a profound effect on wide circles of Soviet intellectuals, made hardly any real political impact on the intellectuals or the industrial workers in the USSR, although the Polish events certainly evoked great interest. When martial law was declared in Poland in December 1981 only one small group, the Young Socialists, which was essentially a clandestine organization, circulated 150 or 200 leaflets in the center of Moscow expressing solidarity with Solidarnosc. All of these Young Socialists were soon arrested, and they all recanted so quickly that the authorities considered it feasible to release them under a partial amnesty, sentencing only one member of the group. (He had refused to give evidence against his friends and collaborators).

In the fall of 1982 several members of the Moscow Group to Promote Compliance with the Helsinki Accords [commonly referred to as the Hel-

sinki Monitoring Group, or Helsinki Watch Group] made the announce-
ment that they were dissolving their organization and ending their activity. This attracted much attention in the Western press, and many Western
observers commented at that time on the disastrous situation the dissident movement found itself in. In the summer of 1982 Vitaly Fedorchuk,
the new chairman of the KGB, stated at a press conference that his organization no longer considered the dissidents a serious danger. "Only
fifteen or twenty of them are still at liberty, and we could arrest them
all in one day." Even as he was speaking, however, social discontent in
the USSR was growing in virtually every part of the population—among
the workers, peasants, intellectuals, and even among lower and middle-
level officials.

Soviet citizens were dissatisfied with the worsening food situation, the
countless cases of waste and mismanagement, and the glaringly evident
increase in all forms and varieties of crime, especially corruption. If public
opinion polls were taken in the USSR, and indexes of the popularity of
various administrations were compiled, the data would likely have shown
that in the summer of 1982 the government's popularity was at its lowest
point in twenty years. This increase in social discontent may partly explain the greater persecution of dissidents. The movement was never truly
a mass movement, but the authorities were trying to completely exclude
the possibility of such a movement in the future.

Repression was not the only factor hurting the movement, however.
Severe blows had been struck at the dissidents in the 1960s and 1970s,
but at that time repression often resulted in more protests and greater
support for the movement. The arrests and searches of people's homes
in the spring and summer of 1982 and the many instances in which
prominent intellectuals were forced to emigrate were accompanied by
hardly any protests at all. This in itself points to a crisis within the
movement which has more than one cause.

In 1970 Sakharov spoke of the possible democratization of Soviet society within four or five years at the most. This prediction of course has
not come true after fifteen years, let alone five. Sakharov himself has
spent more than five years in exile in Gorky under constant humiliating
surveillance by the regular police and the KGB. In 1973 Solzhenitsyn
considered a "moral revolution" in the USSR possible. He even conjectured that such a revolution could occur within a few months. In the

minds of Solzhenitsyn and his co-thinkers such illusions have long since been dispelled. The struggle for the democratization and moral renewal of Soviet society has proven to be a quite prolonged and difficult process. Without producing tangible results, this effort has taken a considerable toll. This has caused disillusion and demoralization and has led many to abandon the movement. They were not prepared for a protracted struggle and severe repression.

It is well known that under heavy pressure from the authorities many of the famous dissidents have taken the road of emigration. Today in the United States, France, Germany, England, Italy, Canada, and Israel there are many more prominent dissidents than remain in the USSR itself, including those in Soviet prisons, camps, and places of internal exile. Among the emigres there are many who thought they could have a better life or more successful career in the West, but only a small minority have succeeded in those aims. The dissidents who were truly devoted to their ideas and principles thought they could maintain their ties with their friends and the movement in the USSR and give help and support from abroad by word and deed. Many interesting works, both fiction and nonfiction, have been published in the West with such aims in mind. Many new Russian-language magazines have also appeared, and the number is still growing.

I have written elsewhere that Samizdat has virtually ceased to circulate in the Soviet Union, and it is not surprising that many have placed their hopes in what is called Tamizdat—that is, Russian-language books and magazines published abroad ("Tam" meaning "over there"). However, these hopes have been realized only to a small extent. First of all, the authorities managed rather effectively to close most of the channels by which such literature entered the USSR. In addition the milieu interested in obtaining such literature has shrunk, partly because of repression and partly because of the general decline of the movement. The content of the literature published in the West also has something to do with the limited circulation of Tamizdat. Many declarations, articles, and fictional works by prominent figures in the "Third Wave" of Russian emigration contain very harsh attacks against socialism in general and even against democracy and liberalism, testifying more than anything to the extreme disillusionment and embitterment of the authors. This content corresponds very little to the attitudes of the oppositionally minded intelligentsia in the USSR, not to mention people who remain to be convinced. Thus, in addition to the difficulties of communication between emigres and dissidents inside the Soviet Union, an ideological gap has arisen and continues to widen. The most vivid example of this is the literary and political activity of Solzhenitsyn, which finds hardly any sympathetic response in his homeland. The same could be said of such figures as Vladimir Maksimov, Pyotr Grigorenko, Vladimir Bukovsky, and Lev Navrozov. There is much more interest in the writings of such varied personalities as Pavel Litvinov, Viktor Nekrasov, Vasily Aksyonov, Valery Chalidze, Efim Etkind, Viktor Perelman (editor of the emigre publication *Vremya i my* [The Times and Ourselves] Andrei Sinyavsky, Lev Kopelev, Naum Korzhavin, Ernst Neizvestny, Aleksandr Zinoviev, and Boris Shragin. The kind of moderation and tolerance of others' opinions that they show has always impressed the intelligentsia here.

Of course disputes, disillusionment, embitterment, and intrigue are typical of all emigre situations, but as one of the leading Polish emigres has said, today's Soviet emigres are really quite exceptional in this regard. That has inevitably had a demoralizing effect on the dissidents remaining in the USSR. Many of us read with interest the few Russian-language publication *Vremya i my* [The Times and Ourselves] Andrei Sinyavsky, pathetic response greeted the anthology *Pamyat* (Memory); the same for the magazines *Forum, Tribuna, Strelets* (Archer), and *Strana i mir* (Our Country and the World). The issues of the magazine *Poiski* (Searchings) published in the 1980s have not aroused much interest. The magazines *Dialog, Problemy Vostochnoi Evropy* (Problems of Eastern Europe), and *Vnutrennie protivorechiya* (Internal Contradictions), on the other hand, are read with interest. Nevertheless the Russian-language press in the West, divided and obsessed with bitter internal feuding, has not provided much of a stimulus to broaden or enlarge the Soviet dissident movement.

Today not only the dissident movement but Soviet society as a whole is under increased pressure. That is one reason why the movement has virtually ceased to attract people who have won fame and recognition in their own fields. In the 1960s and 1970s many outstanding scientists and scholars, including members of the Soviet Academy of Sciences, took part in the movement. Dozens of popular writers and poets, whose works could be found in almost any Soviet library, also joined, along with prominent musicians, performers of world renown, talented sculptors and painters, Old Bolsheviks, and even some Soviet generals. The direct participation of such people, or their sympathy and support, not only provided the opposition with recognized leaders; it also gave much publicity to the movement, making it extremely difficult for the authorities to take countermeasures. Every "punitive operation" against such figures as Rostropovich, Vishnevskaya, Solzhenitsyn, Sakharov, Grigorenko, Neizvestny, Voinovich, or Nekrasov cost the authorities much time and effort; such moves had to be discussed and decided at the highest levels. Today the situation has changed. In the last few years, with the exception of the writer Georgy Vladimov, hardly anyone from the middle levels of the Soviet Establishment has entered the movement. I leave aside the cases of the stage director Yuri Lyubimov and the film director Andrei Tarkovsky, both of whom recently refused to return to the USSR from trips abroad. They had not previously been considered dissidents, although their influence on critically minded intellectuals and young people was quite significant for fifteen or twenty years. The number of sympathizers, people willing at least to sign a protest statement, has also diminished.

There is no doubt that the movement is even now being replenished by newcomers but they are mostly young people without experience or fame. Between their initial, often sharply expressed acts of protest and the first measures against them little time passes, and not all of them continue on the road of protest and dissent after five, three, or two years of confinement, or even after several interrogations or administrative reprisals. Instead they break with the movement or try to emigrate, or sometimes start collaborating with the authorities.

In response to the increased repression a certain number of illegal (clandestine) groups have arisen in the past three or four years. News of their existence comes only after the arrest of some of their members, after some leaflets or slogans on walls appear, or, as happened in Tbilisi in 1983, after an attempted skyjacking. Among such underground groups are the "Young Socialists," some religious and nationalist groups, and even some young admirers of Hitler. In the 1960s and 1970s, all the main opposition groups sought to function openly and legally, although the government declared them illegal nonetheless.

Not much can be told about the underground groups, since there is little information about them and even the trials of their members often pass unnoticed. Nevertheless it is our opinion that in view of the powerful apparatus of surveillance and investigation in the USSR, any lengthy existence is unlikely for such groups. Many instances of repression from 1981 to 1984 were aimed at small illegal groups consisting mostly of young people, some of whom were even prepared to resort to terrorism.

It is no secret that many Soviet dissidents enjoyed not just sympathy but also considerable support (and not only moral support) from Western organizations, private and governmental, and from the press. There is nothing surprising in this, since the Soviet Union has supported numerous opposition groups in Western countries as part of the political and ideological contest between East and West. The largest degree of support from the West was felt during the Carter administration, which made human rights a priority of U.S. foreign policy. This policy obliged President Carter to condemn, at least in words, many of the repressive regimes in Latin America, Asia, and Africa. The Reagan administration, as everyone knows, fundamentally reordered the priorities of U.S. foreign policy.

Reagan is not particularly concerned with human rights in the world or in the Soviet Union. This change in attitude is reflected in the American press and the Western press in general. This policy shift has provoked a burst of indignation and despair from some Soviet dissidents, as expressed for example in a short Samizdat article by Ada Naidenovich entitled "Convergence of the Beast and the Whore" (Konvergentsia zverya i bludnitsy). Her wrath descends first of all upon the Western diplomats and journalists accredited to Moscow, "these emissaries from the free world, in whose persons we have been accustomed to search greedily for the seeds of human dignity and the valor of the undisfigured human spirit. We have gone much too far in idealizing these emissaries. The paradoxical fact is that until American policy 'girded up its loins' with the spiritual weapon of human rights, the behavior of American correspondents was much better, more energetic and courageous. Now they are nothing but a handful of rabbits, afraid of their own shadows.

After all, if you're going to back away in the face of the Beast, you might as well besmirch your own sense of dignity too."

Naidenovich argues that "those who see the USSR and the West as antipodes are mistaken." No, she says, "here we have a symbiosis, a profoundly spiritual union, a fundamental kinship. . . . Who can imagine any real antagonism after seeing how the representatives of these two worlds embrace one another at banquets and grin at each other from ear to ear at diplomatic receptions. How lustfully they engage in the exchange of writers, poets, artists, and officials. How for sixty years whorish Western capital has offered its corpulent udder to the Beast, which draws sustenance from it in the form of loans, credits, and manufacturing licenses. . . . All decent people are tragically alone, they have nowhere to lay down their heads, nowhere to seek consolation. In the church? Alas, God's House on Earth is no less a wasteland than anything else. What is to be done? What is to be done?"

Naidenovich's arguments are hardly worth refuting. Her article has no logic or common sense. She is merely expressing her despair, along with the conviction that the only decent people are people like herself; all the rest, whether in our country or abroad, in politics, the press, or the church, are cowards and scoundrels, who do not wish or are afraid to take the road she has chosen, a road which she herself knows can lead, under present circumstances, only to prison. If there is a certain logic here, it is the upside-down logic of obscuratism and impatience typical of many dissidents today.

Unfortunately such moods have produced works bordering on the pathological in some emigre publications. An example is the long article entitled "The Benefactors" (Blagodeteli) published in the New York Russian-language magazine *Novy Zhurnal* (1982) (no. 147, pp. 198–244). This article informs us that Cecil Rhodes, the promoter of British expansion in Africa, founded a secret Society of the Round Table with the aim of establishing a world government led by the English. After Rhodes' death the society was headed by Alfred Milner, one of the chief financiers "behind the Bolshevik coup." On this model a thick network of secret societies of big capitalists and politicians has grown up in the West, such as the Institute for International Relatins and the Trilateral Commission, which control international finance and banking. Their aim is to forge "an alliance with the Communists and establish a world government." Solzhenitsyn is wrong, the article asserts, when he says that Communism is not understood in the West. It is understood and accepted, but it is being introduced in the United States and Western Europe secretly "through the multimillionaires' associations and the United Nations, which was founded by the Benefactors." The article includes CIA chief William Casey and Defense Secretary Caspar Weinberger among the ominous benefactors.

> All the main U.S. newspapers and all Western magazines are controlled by the secret societies of financiers. They train an enormous number of prominent journalists, politicians, and professors, who promote the ideas of socialism and Marxism. . . . The capitalists' aim is to increase the economic efficiency of the Communist system. . . . If the "big whales" among these benefactors of mankind include the Council on Foreign Relations, the Bilderberg Society, and the Trilateral Commission, there is a multiplicity of other seemingly independent groups and organizations, both open and secret, which are linked with the "whales" by a common purpose and apparently by a common leadership. For example, the American Committee for East-West Accord, headed by Princeton Professor Stephen F. Cohen.

Writing like this may seem delirious, but it is not entirely harmless. Those who established the Third Reich thought along similar lines.

Unfortunately, the mistaken orientation which looked to the West for salvation (and which has ended in disillusion and embitterment) was introduced long ago by Andrei Sakharov. For example, in an interview published in *Le Matin*, September 14, 1978, he said: "As for the future, we do not have great hopes. We do not have any possibilities for changing the situation in which we live, but we can talk about it. To inform public opinion is our only possibility. It is you who must respond. The Western governments must try to obtain concrete results."

For my part, I do not deny the importance of world public opinion, but I think that Sakharov was mistaken in regard to the possibilities actually open to Western govenments. These he obviously exaggerated. In regard to the internal possibilities open to the democratic movement in the USSR, he obviously made an underestimation (although not long before, he had greatly overestimated them). The only social movement in the Soviet Union that can count on at least partial success is one that relies on the moods and trends among groups and social strata within the country that have an interest in change. The number of such groups is really not all that small.

The "victory" of the powerful Soviet machinery of state over the disparate and not very numerous dissident groups, the embryos of political, national, and religious opposition movements, cannot in any way further the development of socialist democracy in the USSR. Such a "victory" cannot help to make public life more animated, create independent social institutions, or increase social control over the agencies of government. Opposition, to be sure, disturbs the often peaceful life of those in power, but it is vitally important in order to restore the health of Soviet society and of the Communist Party itself.

The changes in the party and government leadership since November 1982 have attracted a great deal of attention. People watched closely not only for shifts in accent in Soviet foreign and domestic policy as well as in economic and administrative spheres; much attention has focused also on the attitude the new leadership would take toward the dissident movement. Of course this question was of interest above all to the dissidents themselves. The changes of leadership aroused certain hopes in dissident circles—hopes that were shared by some of the creative intelligentsia, who expected a display of liberalism by the new leaders. Andropov himself had headed the KGB from 1967 to 1982; a new Politburo member, Geidar Aliev, had come from the KGB; and Fedorchuk, whom Andropov promoted from KGB head to minister of internal affairs (in charge of the MVD), was notorious for his harsh measures against Ukrainian dissidents—all these facts did nothing to dispel those hopes.

The KGB is not an organization that can boast of great sympathy from Soviet citizens, although they duly acknowledge its power and influence. The Soviet press, television, and cinema have made enormous efforts in recent years to promote the image of the "glorious Soviet Chekists," not entirely without results, but no fundamental increase in the KGB's popularity has occurred. It was generally known that the dissident movement, in its initial, surprisingly varied and extensive forms, emerged in the years 1965 to 1966, before Andropov took charge of the KGB. His predecessor Semichastny lost his head and asked the Politburo for permission to arrest five thousand persons. Permission was denied. Andropov did not carry out mass arrests, but his extremely negative attitude toward the dissident movement was well known. In his few public statements he made it emphatically clear that an unrelenting struggle against dissent was one of the main duties of the agency he headed. His attitude toward these "renegades" *(otshchepentsy)* was quite biased and tendentious (see *Pravda*, September 10, 1977, and the collection of Andropov's articles and speeches, *Izbrannye rechi i stat'i*, Moscow, 1983, pp. 145–147).

Nevertheless, within a certain section of the intelligentsia Andropov acquired the reputation of a "secret liberal," who was not fully in control of the KGB, where some of Brezhnev's "Dnepropetrovsk Mafia" held leading positions. The fact is of course that Andropov did direct the campaign against the dissidents. One had the impression that he even deliberately exaggerated the danger of internal opposition in order to increase the status and political weight of the KGB and consequently his own importance and influence in the corridors of power.

Although Andropov headed the KGB longer than any of his predecessors, he succeeded to a greater degree than any of them in keeping his own political reputation separate from the agency he headed. He conducted himself less as a security police official than as a politician assigned by the party to oversee the KGB along with other agencies. There is no doubt that this policy helped secure his victory in the short but sharp struggle for power in 1982.

After November 1982 some dissidents speculated that the new leader of the Soviet party and state would be more tolerant and liberal because his new position would not bind him so closely to the KGB. Other observers conjectured that the liberalism of the new Politburo would not go beyond a few symbolic steps—ending the exile of Sakharov and releasing some political prisoners. Pavel Litvinov, for example, had this to say:

Andropov is quite opportunistic. He can go either way. . . . If Andropov wants to show good will toward the West, he should . . . release Andrei Sakharov from exile in Gorky and grant amnesty to leading dissidents still in prison, like Yuri Orlov and Anatoly Shcharansky. These moves would show he is flexible and wants change. It is possible Andropov will move in this direction. (*Newsweek*, November 22, 1982)

Vladimir Bukovsky, who is usually inclined toward extreme formulations, told *Newsweek* (same issue):

> [Andropov] is more intelligent than the others, and . . . we can expect him to be more successful. What I guess is that he will try to relax the ideological rift with the Western left in order to increase his influence abroad. . . . One of the problems he faces is the tarnished image of the Soviet Union among Western left-wingers. But Andropov is a clever guy, and he will try to improve his image. In the first six months to a year he will be sensitive to increasing pressure, especially on the human-rights front, since as the former head of the KGB, he is a very easy target.

These predictions did not come true. The amnesty declared on the sixth anniversary of the formation of the USSR (in December 1982) was not extended to political prisoners, not even those sentenced to relatively short terms. Nor did it apply to religious dissidents or those with only a few months of their sentences remaining. Not surprisingly, the amnesty decree noticeably reduced illusions about the possible liberalism of the new leadership. In addition, on Andropov's initiative, Jewish emigration from the USSR was virtually ended, and the emigration of Soviet Germans, Armenians, and several other national groups was sharply curtailed. It was officially announced that the task of reuniting separated families (an obligation under the Helsinki accords) had for all practical purposes been completed. From November 1982 to November 1984 no more than a thousand families were allowed to emigrate, ten or fifteen times fewer than the average number for a comparable time period in the 1970s.

Andropov took a number of drastic measures aimed at reducing popular discontent. He began a determined campaign against corruption, which affected many influential party and government officials as well as major figures in the black market and the world of underground business operations that exists in the USSR. Increased supervision over local officials was introduced, especially the police and the procuracy.* A number of important decisions were aimed at increasing the production of consumer goods and improving services.

* Procuracy—a Soviet government agency responsible for prosecution of criminals, but also having general supervisory powers to ensure observance of the law by government agencies, officials, and citizens.

At the same time the new administration not only failed to relax but actually intensified all forms of pressure against the few remaining dissidents. Such persons were called in to the offices of the KGB or the procuracy and threatened with prosecution if they did not cease their activities. In early 1983 several trials were held of dissidents who had been arrested earlier, among them Z. Krakhmalnikova, editor of a religious anthology, and a "Russian nationalist" writer, L. Borodin. Nearly all the sentences were quite severe. News also came of several trials in camps, in which political prisoners whose terms were expiring were sentenced anew to two or three years. Some of these prisoners could not withstand the pressure and agreed to make public recantations in return for thier release. At about the same time, Georgy Vladimov, one of the most talented Soviet Russian writers, emigrated. New arrests occurred in Moscow and other cities in 1983. Among those arrested was Sergei Khodorovich, administrator of the Russian Social Fund, founded to provide aid for former political prisoners. Also arrested were some members of a small group of scientists and technicians who tried to found a pacifist organization independent of the government and make proposals for "restoring trust between the USA and the USSR."

If the policy toward the dissidents was the most disillusioning aspect of the new leadership's activity, it was also the least astute. People had to a certain extent grown accustomed to the political repression under Brezhnev, so that the new reprisals carried out in 1981 and 1982 were no surprise to Soviet public opinion, the Western press, or human rights groups in many countries. But a new administration in the Soviet Union is watched closely not only by journalists and Soviet specialists but by the diplomatic and political leaders of most countries. In this situation intensified repression against dissidents brought much stronger protests and had broader repercussions in the West than the oganizers of these measures could have supposed.

The policy of increased repression against opposition groups is in glaring contradiction to Soviet foreign policy, whose officially proclaimed goal is to stop the arms race, expand economic and cultural cooperation between countries with differing social systems, and promote mutual understanding among nations having different ideologies and value systems. In carrying out this policy, the Soviet Union hopes not only for negotiations with Western government leaders but also for cooperation with prominent public figures and religious leaders and support from the many organizations and movements that are in opposition to one or another Western government or social system. However, one can hardly expect success among influential social circles in the West while pursuing a policy of suppression of the beginnings of independent public opinion in the USSR. The Soviet policy in this regard is mistaken and short-sighted.

In the last two or three years the Soviet press has substantially increased its criticism of human rights violations in the West. When we are told that things are bad in our country, we reply that in the West things are even worse. When we are told that there is no freedom of opinion or of the press in the USSR, Soviet propaganda replies that unemployment in the West is growing, as are the number of homeless people and drug addicts. This kind of trading in accusations will not produce greater trust or mutual understanding. One may agree that Western propaganda is often demagogic, but it is equally demagogic to reply by listing the sins of capitalist society in economic and social areas, while exaggerating the considerable but one-sided achievements of the socialist countries in these areas.

The trend toward increased confrontation between the USSR and its allies, on the one hand, and the NATO countries, on the other, is very alarming. Still it is not irreversible. It has not reached the level of the Cold War (1946–56), though that is really small consolation, because the stakes involved today in achieving an illusory nuclear superiority are incomparably higher than they were twenty-five or thirty-five years ago. In the effort to stop the drift toward a new and even more dangerous "cold war" (and I do not question the sincerity of this effort on either side) one must make use of all opportunities. It would be unrealistic to expect that the USSR would change its policy of support for Vietnam, Cambodia, Cuba, or Nicaragua to suit the West, and it would be equally unrealistic to expect that the United States would alter its policy of support to Israel, Taiwan, South Korea, or West Berlin to suit the Soviet Union or any other country. One can hardly hope that Soviet units would withdraw from Afghanistan without a lengthy process of negotiations and the provision of appropriate guarantees. It would be equally imprudent to hope that the U.S. Navy would abandon the Indian Ocean region or that U.S. troops would be withdrawn from West Germany. But if there is the slightest chance that a liberalization of domestic policy, or even a few purely demonstrative steps, would improve East–West relations, it would be highly irrational not to take that chance.

Unfortunately, the situation for dissidents in the USSR did not improve in 1984. At the beginning of the year a number of new laws and supplements to the criminal codes of the RSFSR and the non-Russian republics were published, not in the mass-circulation press, but in the narrowly departmental publication of the Presidium of the Supreme Soviet. The new laws were signed by Yuri Andropov. For example, an article was introduced making it a criminal offense to "transmit, or gather with the aim of transmitting, economic, scientific-technical, or other information constituting an industrial secret to foreign organizations or their representatives by someone to whom such information was entrusted in the line of duty, at work or in government service, or to whom it became known by other means."

Unquestionably it is necessary to protect not only government secrets but also industrial, or trade, secrets *(sluzhebnye tainy)*. Previously violations of business secrecy were punished by administrative procedures. The new law intensifies the punishment, but it does not give a clear definition of "industrial secret." Moreover, those who made a commitment to keep such information secret are not the only ones punishable; those who acquire the information accidentally, and have no idea that confidentiality is involved, also face punishment.

Dissemination of literature containing "deliberately false information about the Soviet social and governmental system" has long been a criminal offense. It was this arbitrarily interpreted formula that served as the basis for most of the reprisals against dissidents in the 1960s and 1970s. Now the appropriate article of the criminal code has been made more precise, referring to the dissemination of such literature "in written, printed, or other form." Such actions are also punishable if they are "committed with the use of monetary instruments or any other material values received from foreign organizations or persons acting in the interests of such organizations" *(Vedomosti Verkhovnogo Soveta* [Register of the Supreme Soviet], January 1984).

Criticism from a legal point of view could also be directed at the decree of September 13, 1983, which added a new article (Article 188–3) to the criminal code. According to this article, "malicious refusal to comply with the demands of the administration of a corrective-labor institution or any opposition to such administration in the performance of its functions by a person serving a sentence in a place of confinement" is punishable by an additional term of imprisonment of up to three years, and in the case of repeat offenders, up to five years.

It is well known that in earlier times various punishments, often quite severe, were meted out to prisoners while they were serving their sentences. But terms were extended only in cases of escape from prison or the committing of crimes in the place of confinement that would be considered crimes outside of prison (murder, theft, etc.). Now the concept of "crime" has been arbitrarily and immeasurably expanded to include all who run afoul of the authorities, whether through their own fault or for no good reason.

Andropov's death and the new changes in the Soviet government have not improved the position of dissidents in any way. The regimen in the prisons and camps continues to grow harsher. Some dissidents of the 1960s, who refused to take up regular work and engaged mainly in charitable activities, have had their Moscow residence permits taken away. Vera Lashkova, for example, was deported from Moscow and offered a job and housing in a small town of the Leningrad region. Searches and arrests have taken place not only in Moscow but also in many other cities. The search records include the titles of many documents and even small magazines, perhaps giving the illusion that Samizdat continues. But these new oppositional documents have not been circulated inside the Soviet Union, and only a few of them have passed beyond Soviet borders and have been published in the emigre press. Most such documents have very quickly come to the attention of the KGB and served as grounds for new arrests. In the 1960s and 1970s, during trials of dissidents dozens or even hundreds of sympathizers would gather outside the buildings where the trials were held. In 1983–84 such expressions of solidarity were hardly to be seen at all. Measures were intensified to isolate those in internal exile, Sakharov in particular. His wife, Yelena Bonner, was also sentenced to five years exile and denied permission to leave Gorky. Less and less news manages to get out of the camps where political prisoners are held.

In 1984 legislation aimed against contacts between Soviet citizens and foreigners was expanded. Now Soviet citizens who invite foreign visitors to their homes even for one day must obtain advance permission from the local police.

In light of what we have said, the question naturally arises, What are the prospects for the opposition movement in the USSR? Its immediate prospects do not seem particularly encouraging. In Soviet ruling circles there is a growing number who favor modernization in all fields of the economy and in some areas within the social sphere. Today, however, the dogmatists and conservatives (who still predominate in the leadership), and the pragmatists and technocrats as well evince a blatant hostility toward any independent social criticism arising from the citizens themselves, free of control by the agencies of power. None of the groups in the upper circles favors a genuine and effective democratization, and none encourages any deviance from the norm. Tolerance of dissent has never been considered a virtue by Soviet leaders, although only a true socialist democracy, allowing freedom of speech and the press within the broadest bounds, can serve as an extremely important, in fact irreplaceable, lever by which to raise the level of the Soviet economy and culture more quickly, and the prestige of the Soviet state and nation within the world community.

There is no disputing the fact that the dissident movement is now in a state of profound decline. But one may confidently assume that it will not be completely destroyed. In a country like the USSR the development of social thought and consciousness can be slowed, weakened, and atomized; but it cannot be stopped entirely. The complex and contradictory path traveled by the dissident movement in the past twenty years has been accompanied by an accumulation of spiritual values and practical experience which will not be lost, no matter what fate befalls the individuals and groups within the movement. The downturn may last a long time, but not forever. At some new stage the movement will begin to expand and grow again, acquiring new forms, new ideas, new participants, but maintaining a definite continuity.

I am confident that with time my country will take on a new look, one

that will be much more attractive than the one we see today. This will occur as the result of internal efforts. Nevertheless the attention and concern of the democratic press and democratic organizations in the West
in regard to all forms of resistance to totalitarianism in the USSR will
always be an important source of support in the difficult struggle for the
democratization of Soviet society.

Roy Medvedev
Translated by George Saunders

On Soviet Dissent

1

The Matrix of Dissent

PO How can we define the dissident in political terms? What is a Soviet dissident? Let's find the broadest definition possible for the moment so that we can single out his general characteristics without going into the ideological and political differences among the dissidents in the Soviet Union.

RM I'd say that a dissident is someone who disagrees in some measure with the ideological, political, economic, or moral foundation that every society rests on, including the Soviet Union. But he does more than simply disagree and think differently; he openly proclaims his dissent and demonstrates it in one way or another to his compatriots and the state. In other words, he doesn't just complain in private to his wife or close friends. This is the most general description I can give you.

PO Then the two factors that typify the Soviet dissidents are their opposition to the constituted power and their refusal to keep it to themselves, their readiness to broadcast it.

RM From the sociological point of view, I think we can say that the dissident emerges from the discontent of some group or other or some stratum of the population. So far no country or social organization on this earth has ever failed to have its quota of elements disaffected with their society either in its entirety or in some particular aspects, yet who have never lost their faith in the moral, political, religious, and cultural values in which that society takes pride. There are such people in the Soviet Union too, among the workers, the peasants, intellectuals, minorities, and the young.

Most often we find this discontent in the upper and lower segments of the population, while the middle classes are more moderate; they don't feel so deprived. The dissident knows how to formulate his objections better than others, and he will give vent to them by taking forthright action—in the USSR mostly in books, articles, open letters, and statements to the foreign press. Or he will organize small political discussion groups. But he seldom takes part in public demonstrations.

PO Westerners tend to see Soviet dissenters as just a handful of intellectuals, but from what you say, it would seem that every Soviet citizen is a potential dissident for the simple reason that he has complaints to make.

RM Well, both of your conclusions are valid. The dissidents do constitute a relatively small circle, usually alienated from the masses; I'm referring to those individuals who very often verbalize the sentiments of the masses without realizing it. On the whole, yes, they are intellectuals. Nevertheless, the stand they take reflects the feelings of a very significant segment of the population, although probably not the majority.

Of course, every Soviet citizen who is unhappy about something in the system is a potential dissident. But in practice, very few of them associate themselves with the open dissenters because they're afraid of losing their jobs, sometimes their freedom, and exposing themselves to attacks from the press. As a rule, the right of political minorities to formulate and declare their own opinions is not recognized in the USSR; therefore, in this country, if a man disagrees or protests or identifies himself as an active dissident, he and his family run the risk of facing a good deal of trouble and

2

danger. Consequently, only a very few are willing to embark on such an adventure.

A number of writers, artists, film and stage directors, and scientists are deeply disturbed by the limitations imposed by the Soviet authorities on freedom of expression. They resent harsh censorship of their work. They chafe at the absurd hindrances put in their way by the bureau chiefs, the publishers, and the ideological commissions. But most of them are resigned to their dilemma. In spite of their exasperation, they will revise their work to conform to the demands of censorship—or better yet, stow it away in a drawer to wait for more enlightened times. Only a few writers decide to publish abroad and accept the risk of being persecuted for it. In provincial cities, most of the industrial and office workers are dissatisfied with the scarcity of goods, the lack of meat, dairy products, fruit, and medicine. But then, the government forbids strikes and protest demonstrations, so that disturbances like the ones that broke out in Novocherkassk in 1962 are extremely rare.*

PO In substance, then, the artist would like to paint in the way he prefers, the author to write what he believes, the historian to choose for himself whatever subject he wants to research, and so on. But the powers-that-be demand that every canvas must be painted in a stipulated way and every novel written according to government dictates. And the historian is not allowed to deviate from the official approach to history, if that's what he wants to do. Can we say that this is true because there is no division in the USSR between the private and the public individual, with the result that—as Marx said [about censors]—"some servants of the state are transformed into spies of the heart, into omniscient souls, philosophers, theologians, politicians, and Delphic oracles?"

RM You see, in the Soviet realm of artistic creativity—and scientific, too—there's practically no line of demarcation between what's pri-

---

* On June 2, 1962, Novocherkassk was the scene of a mass protest demonstration against increased food prices. Troops fired on the crowd, killing and wounding a great many. Top leaders from Moscow flew in and promised concessions, but severe repression against participants in the protests also ensued.

vate and what's public. If you're keeping a diary, naturally you can write what you please in it. But if your observations should bear any influence over even a restricted circle of people, then you could be accused of spreading ideas that are "alien" or "harmful"—or just "incorrect." And that can land you in trouble.

Here's the nub of the matter. Many individuals turn into dissidents because of this dichotomy between their natural creative impulses and the official ban on expressing them. An author doesn't write a novel only for himself and his family. An artist doesn't paint canvases just to hang them on his walls or, in the best of events, to decorate his friends' apartments. In the USSR, there are no private or independent publishers; they're all employed by the state. All art exhibits are sponsored by the Artists' Union, which is controlled in turn by the Communist Party's ideological organs. In his time, Lysenko prevented a number of scientists—biologists, agronomists, and the like—from carrying out their ideas. But this is only one way of becoming a dissident.

PO What are some others?

RM Well, take Sakharov's biography as an instance. Here we find that when he was engaged in creative work, he had at his disposal everything a Soviet scientist could ask for, including generous funds for the research he was doing. He was awarded every major Soviet honor and decorated twice as a hero of socialist labor. But then he began to protest to the Academy of Sciences because of the wretched conditions that were hampering biological research, then under the control of Lysenko and his disciples, who had been supported in the '30s and '40s by Stalin and by Khrushchev in the '50s. Then Sakharov went on to criticize the attempts to rehabilitate Stalin; and finally, he began to remonstrate against every instance of human rights violations in the USSR that came to his knowledge. A good many of his statements in recent years aren't well thought out or rational, and he has made a lot of mistakes in his political actions—in my opinion, at least; all the same, it wasn't because of any difficulties in his work as a theoretical physicist that he made his protests.

4

I can say the same thing about Valentin Turchin, who founded the Russian section of Amnesty International. Turchin is a brilliant theoretical physicist, who had a splendid career ahead of him in the field of pure science. [But in 1974, after he spoke out in defense of Sakharov, he was dismissed from the research institute where he worked; in 1977 he emigrated to the United States.] One of his colleagues once asked me this rhetorical question: "How can I study the flow of neutrons when my country is violating human rights and Soviet troops are swarming over Czechoslovakia!"

Here we can draw an analogy with conditions in the last century. The Decembrists were all noblemen who belonged to Russia's privileged class;* many of them owned vast estates and a good many serfs. Yet they instigated a rebellion against the autocracy. Again in the nineteenth century, other dissidents, like Alexander Herzen, belonged by birth and wealth to the ruling class. Lenin himself was a noble by birth. I could cite any number of similar examples.

PO I think there's still a third way of becoming a dissident, not quite so noble . . .

RM Unfortunately, Soviet dissidents don't always represent only the best elements of the intelligentsia; a lot of people dissent because they're unhappy with their private or social lives. Many join the ranks out of sheer egocentricity, urging foreign correspondents to broadcast to the whole world their crude proclamations, appeals, and horror stories, full of ferocity.

Then there are writers, poets, and artists of every stripe. The poet Urin has published over twenty volumes of his works without winning success or popularity, yet he was profoundly offended when the Writers' Union declined to commemorate his fiftieth birthday. So he announced publicly through the press that he was resigning from the Union, and his statements were broadcast in Russian to the Soviet people by a foreign radio station that didn't have its facts straight. Once when Urin came to see me, he said

* Decembrists—members of Russian secret societies of the 1820s who in December 1825 led an unsuccessful rising against Tsar Nicholas I; generally considered the forerunners of the radical and revolutionary movements of nineteenth-century Russia.

5

. . . and I quote him verbatim . . . "For many years I've always written what they wanted. No one composed a single poem to honor the Soviet troops that went into Czechoslovakia . . . but I did, and I got my verses published. Now the Writers' Union refuses to give a reception to celebrate my fiftieth birthday. All right, I'll fight them, I'll show them who I am."

Men like him are the worst element among the dissidents and threaten to compromise the whole movement. They're prepared to walk out on it or betray their friends whenever the occasion suits them. That's what happened with Pyotr Yakir and Viktor Krasin. They had become involved in some murky matters; then after their arrests [in early 1972] they gave testimony against dozens of others; and at a press conference for foreign journalists [after their trial in September 1973] they denounced their own past deeds as "crimes" and stigmatized as "anti-Soviet slander" everything they'd said and written as dissidents.

PO I suppose the intelligentsia turn to dissent more readily than the workers do. In other words, they realize more clearly their loss of freedom, they understand better the civil rights they're entitled to, and they can state their complaints with more eloquence.

RM That's right. It's the intellectuals who most often become dissenters. But consider this: even in countries where you have freedom of the press and political pluralism, most leaders of the opposition belong to the intelligentsia. In the West, the intelligentsia usually wins the support of those in opposition—workers, white-collar employees, farmers, businessmen, military men, and so forth. In our country, however, it's extremely difficult for these disparate elements to join forces; therefore the intellectuals are left isolated. Take my own case as an example: no group of young people can ask me to lecture at their institute or university, no labor unit can invite me to their factory or their company's recreation facilities. To do that, first they'd have to ask for the authorization of the party or the party's regional committee.

From 1956 to 1966 they could still get official permission. Solzhenitsyn made public appearances in various research institutes, and scientists in Obninsk, not far from Moscow, held discussion meetings in their homes. The Old Bolshevik A. Snegov, an exceptionally fine orator and energetic party activist—he'd spent fifteen years in Stalin's prison camps—often spoke out against Stalin's crimes, and in several military academies at that. But after 1968—that is, the Prague Spring—it wasn't possible because the government cracked down.

Among the workers there are still people with an average education and average intellectual capacities who somehow or other manage to participate in the dissident movement, but they're isolated, too; they daren't reveal themselves, not even to their fellow workers.*

---

* Since the time of this interview, a number of dissidents among Soviet workers have revealed themselves. On November 5, 1977, members of a "Free Trade Union Association of Soviet Working People" (FTUA, for short) held a press conference for foreign journalists in Moscow. Earlier in 1977 they had issued two open letters to world public opinion. This group was led by Vladimir Klebanov, a former coal miner from Donetsk. In January and February 1978 the group held two more press conferences and issued several more documents to foreign journalists, including a list of 43 open members of the FTUA and 110 "candidate members"; they claimed that 200 other workers were ready to join but wanted their names withheld to protect themselves against the authorities. Reprisals against FTUA leaders came almost immediately. By July 1978 at least ten of them, including Klebanov (arrested on February 7), had been placed in psychiatric hospitals or prisons. (The documents of this group, and information about it, have been published in *Workers Against the Gulag*, London: Pluto Press, 1979.)

At an October 1978 press conference for foreign journalists in Moscow, another group of Soviet workers announced the formation of the Free Interprofessional Association of Workers (Russian initials, SMOT) "incorporating the Free Trade Union Association and the Independent Trade Union, which was formed after Klebanov's arrest." It also claimed 200 members. Vladimir Borisov, a Leningrad worker and active dissident since the 1960s, and eight others, some of them also veteran dissidents, were named as members of the Council of Representatives of SMOT (with advisory powers only). In May 1979 one of the council members was sentenced to five years internal exile—on charges of stealing library books; another was sentenced in June 1979 to two years in a labor camp under Article 190-1; a third was forcibly confined to a psychiatric hospital. At time of writing (October 1979) Borisov and the other five council members were apparently still active, although some SMOT supporters had been arrested or had left the USSR.

The "free trade union" groups have centered their activities on publicizing violations of workers' rights (in regard to job safety, unjustified dismissal, nonpayment of unemployment compensation, disability, or pension benefits, noncompliance by management with the labor code, and other conflicts with management or the government authorities).

According to Zhores Medvedev, the statements and aims of these groups are not circulated among Soviet workers but are mainly oriented toward winning publicity outside the USSR. It is difficult to judge how widely they are known, or how much sympathy they have, among Soviet workers in general.

7

PO In other words, the workers are discontented for practical reasons, mainly economic—low salaries, the lack of commodities, services, and the like—while the intellectuals are discontented for ideological reasons.

RM As a rule, yes. Workers rarely generalize about the scarcity of meat or sausage or fruit in their nearby food stores, whereas the intellectuals theorize. Moscow is much better supplied with these necessities than other cities, yet there are more dissatisfied intellectuals in the capital than anywhere else.

PO The government tells us that no bonds exist between the ordinary citizens and the dissidents. Is that because they speak two altogether different languages or is it simply a question of two different ways of showing opposition?

RM I've already said that there are practically no links between the dissidents and the masses. That's not because of any wide gap in the two levels of education and culture but because no end of curbs and limitations prevent dissenters from making direct contact with the people. All mass media in the USSR are monopolized by a single party and the state, don't forget.

The dissidents' generalizations and concepts, in all their various trends, aren't so complicated that other people can't understand them—simple workers, peasants, clerks, teachers, doctors, engineers . . . Of course, some philosophical, political, and sociological concepts are addressed for the most part to the Russian intelligentsia, but even here, the dissidents have no real public, because their books, essays, and appeals are published only abroad, and reach but a few among the intelligentsia. A large number of literary works by dissident writers that deal with political issues, as well as films and plays of that kind, would easily be grasped by the masses—if the authorities allowed their publication. Do you think that only the intellectuals read *One Day in the Life of Ivan Denisovich*, for example?

In the last analysis, intellectuals always create their works for everyone, and it's not their fault if much of what they do is consigned unrealized to their desk drawers. Recently, a Soviet author,

Georgy Vladimov, published a first-rate novel abroad, *The Faithful Ruslan,* one of the best literary works in the last few years. But the Soviet people are denied the privilege of reading it. A trilogy by Eugenia Ginzburg, another marvelous work, will soon come out in Italy.* Had it been published in the Soviet Union at the right time, it would have helped not only the intelligentsia but millions of others to acquire a deeper insight into things.

Authors are better off than other intellectuals because they can put their ideas down on paper and then wait for better times to present them to the Soviet public or send them to publishers in other countries. But film directors can't get to producers abroad, so they have to store their ideas in their heads. I know many of them who have magnificent screenplays in mind but entertain no illusions that they can transfer them to the screen because of censorship.

PO Let's try to imagine the unimaginable. If the men in power put to you the same question that Lenin asked—what is to be done?—how would you answer?

RM I'd say: let the people know about these concepts, let the people discuss them and reach their own conclusions. The men in power persist in treating the laborers, the peasants, the white-collar workers, and the great mass of non-manual workers like immature children, who must be safeguarded against evil ideological influences. Thus, they impoverish the nation's moral consciousness, they fail to educate the people and prepare them for real political maturity . . . and that in an age like ours when the world is more and more open to new ideas, to the circulation of ideas and information regardless of national frontiers.

PO Do people in general have a "thirst" for information?

---

* Eugenia Ginzburg was a loyal Communist Party member arrested and sent to Stalin's camps in 1937. The reference is to her memoirs of the camps, published in a three-volume edition by Mondadori. The first part of the memoirs circulated widely in samizdat in the mid-1960s and was published in many languages, the English version (1967) being entitled *Journey Into the Whirlwind.* Ginzburg subsequently expanded the work, adding two volumes of material on the years 1940–1956.

9

RM   Sometimes workers in Moscow or from the provinces come to me for information, but I can't possibly expound my ideas or explain the various currents dividing the Moscow dissidents to all of them, each one separately. Almost every one of my visitors asks me for something to read, for himself or his friends. But I don't run a public library or a warehouse of books at home, so many of them go away disappointed.

In the last few years, a number of people, especially from the provinces, have tried to see Sakharov, but neither can he receive more than a small fraction of them; and, because some of them cannot understand why, occasionally curious things happen. One worker slept in the waiting room at the railroad station for several nights, and still he couldn't get to Sakharov. Finally he got hold of his telephone number and rang him late one night, only to be told by Sakharov's wife that he couldn't come to the telephone because he was taking a bath. The next day the worker came to me, indignant because Sakharov could take a bath while people slept in the railroad station waiting to see him!

Unfortunately, I too am obliged to turn down many would-be callers, nor can I reply in detail to the dozens of questions people ask in the letters they write me. But we have to raise these barriers in self-protection, you can't blame us for it.

PO   One inclines to believe that if all dictators knew the thoughts and problems of their people, they wouldn't hesitate to meet their demands. But they're in the dark about these things because the bureaucracy withholds such information from them. Is that true in the USSR?

RM   No. It's not true that our men in power don't know everything people think or the viewpoints of the masses, or that the power system in the Soviet Union has no feedback. The party organizations and the local soviet units keep the men at the top well informed on what the masses are thinking; certainly they're better informed than the dissidents are. They're notified immediately whenever an incident of any consequence occurs in the provinces, such as spontaneous strikes, the explosion of rudimentary bombs, and all mass

10

demonstrations. The dissidents never hear about such things nor, certainly, do the foreign correspondents, with good reason.

For instance, who heard about the strike in Tula, when the workers in some of the factories there stayed on the job but refused to collect their salaries because, they said, there wasn't anything to buy? Or who could have known about the Leningrad taxi drivers' strike against the government-fixed fare hike, which had caused people to virtually stop taking taxis altogether? The authorities in Moscow are instantly alerted to all such incidents.

PO Why is the Kremlin so anxious to raise barriers between the dissidents and the rest of the population?

RM Because the bosses are afraid that easy, widespread contacts might induce people to organize small parties or political groups opposed in their principles and structure to the Communist Party of the Soviet Union (CPSU). Our society is in the embryonic stages of an evolution into pluralism; it is not destined always to remain homogeneous, as it is today. Yet the men in the saddle fear rising opposition without realizing that, in most cases, opposition would be most useful to them. It means a healthy society, whereas total consensus indicates an ailing society. Pluralism is the natural corollary of a developed socialism; where it doesn't exist, you have an immature society.

PO Most of the Soviet population learns about what's happening in their own country and elsewhere from foreign radio broadcasts . . . also what the dissidents are up to. Would you say that these broadcasts stimulate the people? I mean, do they encourage them to formulate their own critical viewpoints as they acquire more knowledge, and thereby add to the ranks of the dissidents?

RM Without any doubt, foreign news reports provide an important source of information for the Soviet people. Experts calculate that about one-fourth of the adults in the cities listen to them, but I think this estimate is exaggerated: those who listen regularly, not just from time to time, are many fewer. Anyway, these broadcasts are certainly an important contributing factor to the nation's ideo-

11

logical life because people who hear them pass on the information to their friends and relatives. The newscasters put a good deal of emphasis on the dissident movement, which influences the listener's thinking and opens the way to more dissent, but only on a very small scale.

On the other hand, Western news broadcasts sometimes distort the facts about life in the USSR, about the dissidents' activities, and the current situation in the Western countries. Nevertheless, it's most important that every individual should have the right to turn the dial on his radio set and acquaint himself with the opinions of the American press, the Western European press, and the comments of specialists on the different trends and the significance of some particular event, just as he should know what the Chinese propagandists have to say . . . although from what I can make out, no one cares about listening to the Chinese radio—better to switch to another station.

PO   The fact remains that while the Russian dissidents in the nineteenth century—the Decembrists and populists—were wholly isolated from the masses because they had no means of communicating with them, your dissidents today are not, at least not altogether. I'd like to ask this question: would it be possible for the foreign radio to go beyond its function of disseminating information to mobilize the masses on the side of dissent, that is to serve as a rallying point for bringing democracy to the Soviet Union?

RM   Well, you see, our people can pick up not only American, British, and West German stations but also those of a number of other countries: France, Israel, Iraq, Egypt, Japan, India, Canada, Sweden, therefore we aren't by any means cut off from the global flow of information and ideas. But it's too early to talk about bringing democracy to the Soviet Union.

As I've said, an active dissident runs serious risks. The majority of people who listen to foreign broadcasts are certainly eager to hear news about the dissidents and discussions of their movement, but Soviet listeners are like the ancient Roman spectators who sat in the Coliseum and watched the show in the arena. The Romans cheered the gladiators who displayed the most courage and skill,

12

but not many chose to go into the arena themselves to do combat with the gladiators or wrestle with the wild beasts.

PO Then you don't believe that this flood of information will contribute in any way toward destabilization of the system.

RM I couldn't say for sure. First, we mustn't overestimate the impact it makes. Even those Soviet citizens who read English, German, or French, and listen regularly to foreign news broadcasts don't always have enough information on major international events. It's very hard for us to find serious reading material on political science, sociology, and philosophy published in the West—and no radio can substitute for this source of information. We have no possibility of reading foreign newspapers and magazines with any regularity. In Moscow, even Communist publications from the West go on sale only intermittently. And let's not even mention the snags that disrupt our postal service.

But even if these obstacles to a free exchange of information and ideas should suddenly disappear, there's no guarantee that it would destabilize Soviet power. To the contrary, it would consolidate Soviet power and render it more attractive and flexible. It would make it possible to distinguish between socialism as a political system and Soviet power, between the governmental structure of socialist society in general and the particular regime that now rules the USSR, which is only one variant . . . and not the best, by far . . . of state socialism.

PO Would you clarify that?

RM Socialism and Soviet power have the potential capacity to refute any criticism from the West because, theoretically, socialism represents a higher stage of human advancement than capitalism does. The Soviet Union hasn't yet achieved advanced socialism, only a complex mixture of socialism and pseudo-socialism. Therefore, the flood of information from abroad cannot damage socialism per se but only that dogmatic, bureaucratic, malformed regime which still retains some elements that allow us to call it a socialist and Soviet society, in spite of all its imperfections.

Even if the Western propaganda mills that feed their radio out-

13

lets do attack the socialist system, their broadcasts can in effect
spur its development because the evolution of the Soviet people's
civil liberties and their expanding individual freedoms won't lead
to destabilization but to the very opposite: the reinforcement and
progress of socialism.

Speaking generally, information can have considerable effect on
a regime. The form of rule that was based on the cult of Stalin
collapsed after the Twentieth Congress,* and since then no efforts
to restore it have succeeded. Information can swiftly demolish the
reputation of a political boss, it can disprove false and dogmatic
tenets, but information and propaganda alone won't wipe out a political system, not even an extremely reactionary one. In the West,
how many books and essays have been written over the past two
centuries against capitalism? Yet capitalism is still with us.

* Twentieth Congress of the CPSU, held in Moscow February 14–25, 1956, at which
Khrushchev gave his "secret speech," which, for the first time, officially acknowledged and
denounced some of Stalin's crimes.

2

On being a Dissident

PO Let's go back to the situation of the dissident in the USSR. What changes in his life? What becomes of his family, his work, and his private life when the authorities stamp him as a dissenter?

RM The fate that befalls every dissident is so personal that we cannot generalize. It depends first on where the individual in question lives, whether in Moscow or somewhere in the provinces, on his age, his convictions, his behavior, the degree of his courage, how well-known he is in the USSR and abroad, his social position until the moment he falls into disgrace, and many other factors. I know a simple pharmacist in Vladimir who was sentenced to two years in jail only because he kept a few so-called *samizdat* books and articles in his possession. He had also written some poems and in one of them criticized the invasion of Czechoslovakia.

    Then there's an elderly woman, a member of the Communist Party since 1926, who has been behaving like a dissident for a long time. She has written a number of essays, many of which appeared in various Western publications and in the *Chronicle of Current*

15

Events.* But she's seventy-one years old and ailing; so far she hasn't been persecuted or even expelled from the party. Last year the party sent her a summons—not to expel her, as she feared, but only to offer her a reception in honor of her fifty years as a militant!

A Leningrad physicist, Revolt Pimenov, was sentenced to internal exile for five years for distributing works the tribunal deemed anti-Soviet. Sakharov, the academician, lost his job in the atomic and missile industry but wasn't stripped of his title as academician or fired from his post in another scientific research institute. And during the 1976 trial of the Crimean Tartar leader Mustafa Dzhemilev at a courthouse in Omsk, when Sakharov slapped a major of the militia, the local police authorities did nothing more than detain him briefly and put the offense on record; no other dissident would have gotten off with less than four years in prison.

Some dissidents are thrown into mental institutions while others are allowed to emigrate freely from the USSR. The Crimean Tatar dissidents are worse off than their Jewish counterparts because they don't have strong support from abroad. Pyotr Yakir, who caved in after he was arrested and gave the police all the testimony they wanted to round up many of his friends as traitors, was exiled to Ryazan but soon released.† Vladimir Bukovsky, who was little known in the USSR and outside, spent half his life in prison until the Soviet Union traded him for Luis Corvalan.‡

My brother Zhores lost his job at a scientific institute in Obninsk because he'd written a number of hard-hitting articles for *samizdat*. After a year and a half they committed him to an insane asylum but let him go in three weeks because of a massive protest

---

* An information bulletin that, since April 1968, has appeared regularly and been circulated unofficially (in *samizdat*) in the USSR. It reports facts on violations of basic rights by the Soviet authorities in an objective way and gives news of the civil-rights movement and of uncensored publication in manuscript or other form (*samizdat*). Amnesty International has published an English-language edition since 1971.

† Yakir was given the rather mild sentence of three years internal exile (enforced residence) in Ryazan, not far from Moscow, and pardoned after a year, in September 1974.

‡ Bukovsky was flown to Switzerland in mid-December 1976, and simultaneously—through U.S. government mediation—Chile released Corvalan, general secretary of the Chilean Communist Party, who was flown to Switzerland and went on to Moscow.

from Moscow's intelligentsia. The government then permitted him to resume his scientific career and, in 1973, to accept an invitation to work in a British medical center. But after he had been in England eight months, he was deprived of his Soviet citizenship and forbidden to return to the USSR with his family. I cite these examples to show how differently dissenters can be punished in the Soviet Union.

In 1969, the party threw me out. The next year, according to what I've been told, the authorities thought about arresting me, but my case was deferred. In 1971, the police searched my house and confiscated a good part of my archives, but after I published my two most important books, *Let History Judge* and *On Socialist Democracy*, and the one I wrote with my brother, *A Question of Madness*, they left me in peace. That was five years ago, and I still do my work unmolested; no one bothers my research assistants either. With help from Zhores, who represents me abroad, I'm financially secure. Of course I can't tell what might befall me in the future . . . and this uncertainty impels me to work with heightened intensity. But my situation is an exception to the rule.

In a word, the KGB organs are very eclectic in their methods of repression. Over the past years we have observed a growing preference on the part of the political police to send dissenters out of the country rather than arrest them. But some have stubbornly refused to leave.

PO The government's attitude is very curious. One might call it a combination of sentimentality and realism.

RM Realism yes, but sentimentality no. Nowadays when the government persecutes and arrests the sick and elderly . . . some of them more than seventy years old, and many of them incarcerated in Stalin's jails and prison camps, sometimes for fifteen or eighteen years . . . there's a public outcry, even from people who don't concern themselves with politics, not to mention from friends, relatives, and neighbors.

PO But the government doesn't always follow the same standards of control and repression, and the dissidents must resort to different

17

tactics, depending on prevailing conditions and their individual cases.

RM When I wrote *Let History Judge* in the '60s, to me the most important issues were Stalin's crimes and the phenomenon of Stalinism. I wrote extensively about the guilt of his collaborators, men like Kaganovich, Molotov, Voroshilov, Malenkov . . . yes, and Yezhov, Beria, Vyshinsky, Yagoda, and more. Then several Old Bolsheviks brought me documentation on the crimes committed by Khrushchev and Mikoyan, too, and on Suslov's involvement in various disgraceful ideological campaigns during the '40s. But I didn't incorporate that material in my book, not only because Mikoyan was president of the Presidium of the Supreme Soviet at the time and Khrushchev first secretary of the party, but also because both of them had played decisive roles in exposing Stalin at the Communist Party's Twentieth and Twenty-Second Congresses. Another time I was given documents from the party archives marked "secret," but here again I couldn't use them because I worked on the book openly, I never hid the manuscript away in some dark corner as Solzhenitsyn did, for example, when he was writing *The Gulag Archipelago,** which he intended to have published only after his arrest or his death.

If I'd had secret party documents concealed in my home, that would have given the authorities a good pretext to penalize me with some arbitrary form of repression, and I couldn't have finished the book. So I had to choose the lesser of two evils. That's why the book isn't as complete as it would have been otherwise, but at least I was able to finish it and have it published in almost every European language and even in Japanese.

PO The first sanction usually inflicted on the dissident is dismissal from his job. In this, the Soviet authorities react like the worst of capitalists. In Italy in former times, a man who made no bones

---

* Gulag—acronym for Chief Administration for Corrective-Labor Camps. The term became world-famous with the publication of Solzhenitsyn's three-volume study of the string (or "archipelago") of camps, prisons, etc., under the control of this state agency.

18

about his allegiance to the left and talked about it freely in his place of work, faced the same danger. Don't you find it paradoxical that a state which professes to be socialist should act in the same way as Italian capitalists used to?

RM There were black lists in tsarist Russia too, and a worker couldn't hold a job easily anywhere unless he gave political guarantees. In the Soviet Union the same discrimination is even worse because the state has a total monopoly; it's the nation's only employer. Nevertheless, things aren't the same as they were in Italy years ago or in tsarist Russia; it's more like West Germany's *Berufsverbot*, which prevents employers from hiring "radical elements" for many jobs.

As a rule, Soviet dissidents are not allowed to pursue their intellectual professions, but they can work as simple laborers or clerks or ordinary assistants in the sciences. Some are offered jobs in libraries or archives of secondary importance. A friend of mine, expelled from the party for his oppositional ideas and actions, got a post in the USSR National Library and went to work compiling a catalogue of journals published in Russia and in the Russian Federative Soviet Socialist Republic (RSFSR) between 1917 and 1920.

Some of these penalties have a certain logic. If a man disillusioned with Marxism and socialism proclaims himself an Orthodox Christian, certainly he'll never take over as editor-in-chief of *Pravda* or *Isvestia* or the journal *Nauka i Religia* (Science and Religion). But it makes no sense to fire a good physicist or laboratory chief from some institute engaged in physics research because he objects to the invasion of Czechoslovakia, let's say. And there have been a good many cases like that. I know a young scientist, a top specialist in theoretical physics, who has achieved more positive results in his work than some members of the Academy, yet he's only an assistant now, and he can't put the thesis of his doctorate into practice only because he refused to take the required examination in party history.

PO Since the state is the country's only employer, it forces those who disagree with its policies to quit their careers for some other line of work. Dubček,* for example, was assigned to the office of the forest rangers on the outskirts of Prague. How might a dissident circumvent this kind of logic?

RM I don't know that it was degrading for Dubček to work with the forest rangers in Czechoslovakia, when you have a man like Husak as chief of state.† Would Dubček *want* to be a member of Husak's Central Committee or secretary of any regional party committee today? But obviously, for many dissidents, being denied work in their professions is a serious psychological trauma. The answer to the problem, however, depends mainly on the individual's personal aspirations. If an author is expelled from the Writers' Union, that could prove to be a boon because it frees him not only from official censorship but also from his inclination to censor himself, and he can begin to use his own language to turn out better works than he could have written abiding by the strictures of the Union. A dissenting poet will write much better poetry than another who submits to the demands of the regime. In the past ten years, Yevgeny Yevtushenko has become a really bad poet; his decline began with the state's official recognition of him and with his appointment to the board of the Writers' Union. He wrote his best poetry when he was a semi-dissident. The greatest Russian poets of the past seventy years were Mandelstam, Pasternak, Tsvetaeva, Akhmatova, and Yesenin, all of them dissidents for one reason or another, and all of them subjected to discrimination and repression.

Then there are those who don't work alone but in collaboration with others. A dissident stage or screen director deprived of his profession will find his creativity drying up. A dancer dismissed from his troupe loses the skill of his art. A theoretical physicist can go on working somehow or other after he's been fired, but an experimental physicist without equipment or a laboratory will lose his expertise, and so will an instructor with no students to teach.

---

* Alexander Dubček—head of the Communist Party of Czechoslovakia during the Prague Spring, the 1968 liberalization which was brought to an end by Soviet occupation in August.

† Gustav Husak—replaced Dubček as head of the Czechoslovak Communist Party in April 1969; since then his regime has cooperated closely with the Soviet occupation.

PO With what psychological consequences?

RM Well, a good deal depends on the nature and resilience of the individual's character. Persecution and pressure will humiliate, sometimes destroy, the weak, but toughen others by helping them to develop into strong personalities. In nineteenth-century Russia the creative work of nearly all the great figures came after they had clashed with the power structure and the men who controlled it. They, too, were dissidents, but they transcended their time, although some of them eventually made compromises with the Establishment, as Dostoevsky did and, to a certain extent, Pushkin.

The same thing has happened to scientists in every age when they protested against prevailing political and scientific tenets and endured mortification and persecution as a result. This is because old, entrenched dogmas persist everywhere, and people will defend them tenaciously with every weapon at their command.

So, you see, no one can say that the persecutions in the Soviet Union or in any other country will totally destroy literature, art, and science. Of course, when persecutions reach such appalling levels as they did in the '30s under Stalin and in China over the last fifteen years, neither literature nor science will make much headway, but their development won't be totally arrested.

PO The artist has to confront practical considerations. If the state is the only buyer of art works, how do the dissidents live?

RM I can't give any single reply to your question. Many world-famous Western artists whose works are selling for millions of dollars went unrecognized and unappreciated during their lifetimes, and some of them died in misery. This was true of almost all the Impressionists, Monet, van Gogh, and others. The same happened in earlier times; just remember Rembrandt. The genius of not a few writers wasn't realized until after their death. This is true not only of Bulgakov.* Stendhal, too, was appreciated by only a few con-

---

* Mikhail Bulgakov (1891–1940), Russian novelist and satirical playwright of the 1920s and 1930s, most famous for his *Master and Margarita*, completed in 1938 but published posthumously only in 1966–67.

21

noisseurs while he lived, not by the general public. In fact, much of what he wrote was published posthumously. In any case, a really great writer or painter doesn't think about clients when he creates a work.

Most nonofficial Soviet painters live in very trying circumstances. They sell their canvases to friends or art lovers, sometimes to foreign tourists and diplomats. Many nonofficial writers give their books only to trusted friends to read, others send them to foreign publishers, in which case they retain the author's rights, which aren't as high as one might think. Then, since they live in the Soviet Union, they have a hard time collecting their money. I know a lot of excellent works . . . novels, memoirs, poetry collections . . . that are stored away in bottom drawers.

But there's another side to the story. Not all nonofficial artists . . . or nonconformists, as they call themselves . . . have genuine talent. They often hide behind nonconformity to conceal the fact, so that you have innumerable works by graphomaniacs of every stripe circulating in the USSR along with the works of really fine artists.

PO But those who have no remunerative métier—how do they survive?

RM They have a tough time, of course. Some of them work privately at bookbinding, restoring furniture, doing things like that. Some are helped by their families and friends, not many of whom will refuse to contribute what they can. A Russian proverb says, "No one will hesitate to give thread to make a shirt for a naked man." But we must remember one thing: that in my country everything of prime necessity, like housing, transportation, bread, milk, and so forth, is extremely cheap. And that's an advantage not to be underestimated.

PO When dissidents are sentenced to prison or labor camp, on what basis do the authorities give their verdict?

RM I believe that sending people to jail and prison camps for having ideas of their own and making them known is illegal and senseless, even if some clause or other in the penal code calls for such punishment. Stalin perpetrated any number of cruel laws we now deplore as an abuse of power. Why must a Soviet citizen spend three or four years in confinement because he's thought to be anti-Soviet? And if he dislikes socialism to begin with, will he like it any better after five or seven years of living under the harsh regime of some labor camp?

Stalinist power had a brutal logic all its own. In the Gulag system, no one ever regained freedom; from jail one went to a labor camp, from camp to internal exile. With unabashed cynicism the authorities declared that if people weren't anti-Soviet at the outset, they would certainly become so after doing a stretch in some camp; therefore it was best to keep them imprisoned. Today the terms of the penal code are respected, but that doesn't justify throwing people in prison simply for their ideas. Such a thing is unacceptable in any country that calls itself democratic.

We mustn't forget that there were political prisoners in Khrushchev's time too, although most of them were released after the Twentieth Congress. But after the Hungarian uprising in 1956, dozens of young people who demonstrated against Soviet suppression of the revolt in Budapest wound up in jail or in prison camps. The regime persisted in thinking that anyone who opposed the party in a crisis of such magnitude must be punished.

This was the standard Stalinist logic, but it began to break down after Sinyavsky and Daniel were put on trial,* mainly for the ideas they expounded in their creative writings. The reaction that trial aroused throughout the USSR and abroad was so vehement that not even the most obtuse could ignore it. Gradually the system changed, and became more flexible.

PO How did the change work in practice?

---

* The trial of Sinyavsky and Daniel in February 1966 marked the beginning of an official drive to curb dissent; it provoked protests that gave rise to the democratic movement of the 1960s and 1970s. They were singled out for their satirical, anti-Stalinist works published outside the USSR under pseudonyms (Abram Tertz for Sinyavsky, Nikolai Arzhak for Daniel). Sinyavsky was given seven years in a labor camp; released in early June 1971, he emigrated and now lives in Paris. Daniel's sentence was five years in the camps, where he was active in prisoners' protests; released in September 1970, he now lives in the Moscow area.

RM   Recently a dissident who'd spent ten years in a camp gave a lecture for his circle of friends on a highly original theme: Why someone ends up in a camp. From his observations he concluded that in recent years, most of the people sentenced to the camps were persons of weak character, whom the authorities hoped to bend to their will and, in fact, often did. They didn't arrest those they thought couldn't be "straightened out" in the camps; instead they resorted to other repressive measures—in the past few years mainly forced emigration.

   Dissidents suffer persecution far more than people imagine, not only on the basis of Articles 70 and 190 of the RSFSR penal code* but all the other articles as well, by which they're accused of violating the law in all sorts of ways. The imputations are often downright absurd. A prospective victim can be indicted for speculation, violation of currency regulations, or "petty hooliganism," a label sometimes applied to a citizen's attempt to enter the premises of a foreign embassy. The police have punished dissidents severely for disobeying the rule that forbids unauthorized persons to take up residence in Moscow, although thousands of others transgress it with impunity.

---

* Article 70 forbids "agitation or propaganda carried on for the purpose of subverting or weakening Soviet authority or of committing especially dangerous crimes against the state, or the [verbal] spreading for the same purpose of slanderous fabrications which defame the Soviet political and social system, or the circulation or preparation or keeping for the same purpose, of literature of such content"; it carries penalties of up to seven years imprisonment with an additional term of up to five years internal exile.

Article 190 (clause 1) forbids "anti-Soviet slander"—or literally, oral or written "dissemination of fabrications known to be false which defame the Soviet political and social system"; it carries a maximum penalty of three years confinement in a prison or labor camp.

3

The Trial

PO Let's talk about your own case—your expulsion from the party. How did that happen?

RM Ah, that's an old story . . a long one, and not very interesting now. It had to do mostly with my book *Let History Judge.* I began writing it in 1962 and finished the first draft in 1964, when I showed it to various Old Bolsheviks, writers, and others who could help me with it. Twice within one year I rewrote the text entirely. I hadn't given out many copies of the manuscript, yet a lot of people knew what the subject was. In 1966 Tvardovsky read it, also members of the *Novy Mir* board, in 1967 Academician Sakharov and a few of his friends. Some of my acquaintances on the Central Committee heard about it, and it was no secret to the KBG.*

But then, toward the end of 1967, while the police were searching the home of my friend I. Nikolaev in Leningrad, they found a copy of the book, which ran to almost one thousand pages. So I sent it to the Central Committee, pointing out that it was a work

---

* KGB—initials of the Soviet security police since 1954, the Komitet Gosudarstvennoi Bezopasnosti, or Committee of State Security. Before that the security agencies were known by various acronyms or initials: the Cheka, 1917–21; GPU or OGPU, until 1934; NKVD or NKGB, 1934–46; and MGB or MVD, 1946–54.

still in progress. They sent it on to Vladimir Stepakov, who was then the head of the Central Committee's department of agitation and propaganda; from there it somehow fell into the hands of the department of education of the party's Moscow city committee, probably because I was then working at the Academy of Pedagogical Sciences, a scholar institute in Moscow.

At that point, someone from a publishing house that issues political tracts came to see me and asked for a copy to read. I gave it to him, of course, but explained that it was only the first draft. After six months, the manuscript was returned to me with a cryptic note. Until 1969, however, the authorities made no attempt to stop me from continuing to work on the book. But in that year, everything changed.

PO   What happened?

RM   That was the year of Stalin's ninetieth birthday . . . He was born in December, but many influential Stalinists launched a campaign to rehabilitate him even earlier. They managed to obtain a resolution, probably on the level of a Central Committee secretaryship, that would have meant at least a partial rehabilitation. *Pravda* featured a leading editorial on him, and the Institute of Marxism-Leninism dedicated a scientific session to him and compiled a selection of his works for publication. Also, there was a plan afoot to sell portraits and busts of him. The resolution, no doubt under the heading "miscellaneous," pointed out the necessity of expelling the most vocal critics of the Stalin cult, the Old Bolshevik A. V. Snegov, myself, and others. It was certainly no coincidence that General Pyotr Grigorenko was arrested in 1969 and committed to a mental institution.

In February and March, *Kommunist,* the official organ of the Central Committee, ran two articles extolling Stalin. That signaled the opening of a pro-Stalin campaign. I decided I had to reply to it in some manner. In April I wrote a long open letter to the editors of *Kommunist* and sent copies of it to all the members of the Politburo and a number of the intelligentsia in Moscow. With my con-

sent, the text was published in France in the form of a pamphlet.*
I also sent a copy of *Let History Judge* to friends in Paris to safeguard for me.

Back in Moscow after my summer holiday, my local committee
immediately summoned me to appear before it and expelled me
from the party. Their justification appeared in a two-page report
(*spravka*) which evaluated my book in malicious, defamatory language. Without citing any proof whatever, the report stated that I
considered erroneous everything the party had done between 1920
and 1940, that I denied it was building socialism in our country,
that I borrowed my views mainly from bourgeois sources, that I
had maligned the party's achievements in strengthening the army
and preparing the nation for war, and other charges. In conclu-
sion, it said that "on the pretext of criticizing the cult of Stalin, I
had defamed the entire Soviet people, together with the state and
social system."†

PO But Stalin wasn't rehabilitated after all.

RM No, neither in 1969 nor after—although, mind you, the danger was
very real. There was no celebration of his ninetieth birthday and
Pravda never published that special editorial; instead, it ran a
brief notice in an altogether different style. Of course, some
members of the Politburo probably felt that rehabilitating Stalin
wouldn't be correct and certainly not timely; but the principal factor that forestalled it was the intervention of several Western Communist leaders in behind-the-scenes disputes.

I'm told that in mid-December 1969, Gomulka, Kadar, and
Longo,‡ all three on an official visit to Moscow, firmly declared
that they couldn't in any way support the move to rehabilitate
Stalin, and that they would be obliged to keep their distance themselves from any such move if the Soviet Communist Party insisted

* *Faut-il rehabiliter Staline* (Paris, 1969).
† Implying a possible criminal offense under Article 190.
‡ Wladyslaw Gomulka, Janos Kadar, and Luigi Longo—leaders, respectively, of the Polish,
Hungarian, and Italian Communist parties.

on going ahead with it. At the time, relations between the Soviet and various other Communist parties were somewhat strained. Just a short time before, the Soviets had succeeded . . . but only with great difficulty . . . in holding an international conference of the different parties in Moscow, and few of our leaders were willing to risk another rupture with them. That's why it was agreed . . . by a majority but not a unanimous vote . . . to call off the rehabilitation plan.

Going back to my own story, in the autumn of 1969 I signaled friends abroad to make the necessary contacts toward getting my book published outside the USSR. At the end of that year I signed a contract with the American publisher Knopf, who gave out the text for translation. Among the terms of the contract I stipulated that Knopf must not give the book any publicity before issuing it in 1971.

PO   What is the procedure for expelling a member of the party? Does the defendant have recourse to any higher political body?

RM   The procedure is fixed by party statutes. In my case, however, some of the statute clauses were unquestionably violated. First of all, it was never brought up for debate in the basic party organization to which I belonged, that is in the institute where I was working. I believe that the responsible men on my local committee probably feared that many of my colleagues would defend me, and that would compromise the ultimate verdict in the "Medvedev case."

As I said, the local committee never put the matter to a debate or discussion; the presiding officer of the appointed commission simply read aloud an official report on my book. When I asked who the author of it was and pointed out that a scientific work must be discussed in a scientific organization, my objections fell on deaf ears. And although my manuscript lay on the committee secretary's desk, not one of the local leaders had read it or so much as leafed through it. One of them told me in an arrogant tone, "I have never read books of that kind nor will I ever read them." The session lasted no more than twenty minutes, and at the end, the committee secretary announced that since Roy Medvedev did not

28

confess his errors or retract his wrong ideas, the party had no
choice but to expel him.

Of course I appealed to the Moscow city committee, and there
the procedure was practically the same. A good number of Old
Bolsheviks had written the committee a collective letter, but it
wasn't even read during the session, and no old party member was
invited to attend the trial. To answer a new report on my book
written by two collaborators of the Moscow Party's Institute of
History, I was permitted to speak for ten minutes, more or less.
But no one on the city committee had read my manuscript either,
and the members hastily approved the decision to expel me "for
the incompatibility of my ideas with membership in the party."
This occurred in October 1969.

Whereupon I submitted an appeal to the Central Committee's
Control Commission. There things went differently. You see, the
local and city committees are concerned with administrative and
organizational matters, so that a case of expulsion from the party
is only an occasional minor question they want to settle without
losing too much time. But the Central Committee's Control Commission is mainly concerned with personal cases of party members,
so that it gives more attention to them. Each case is examined by
one or two party investigators. I had two of them. Both had read
my manuscript, and they summoned me time and again for discussions that lasted for hours.

PO   What happened at those discussions?

RM   Well, I'll quote a few passages from the transcript.

> Investigator: On what grounds did you presume you had the right to
> examine and analyze the events of our history on your own initiative?
> Who authorized you to write a book on Stalin?
> Roy Medvedev: I had no such authorization, and this was not one of
> my official duties. But history, including the history of the party,
> belongs to no one; there's no monopoly on it. Therefore I haven't
> presumed anything. No one can deny me the right to express my opin-
> ion on any event in history, whether you like it or not. I don't have to
> ask anyone's permission.
> Investigator: But you're a party member, and you know that we
> have institutes that specialize in the history of the party with all the

29

necessary materials and documents at their disposal. You're an instructor, your job is to teach your students.

Roy Medvedev: Yes, and when the Moscow bakers bake good bread, no housewife thinks of kneading her own, as they used to do in the country. If I felt that our history institutes really studied the nature and history of Stalinism and Stalin's crimes, I wouldn't have written my book. But I know that they don't do any research on that subject. And while they have a good deal of material and many documents at their command, they don't examine or analyze them. Now they're trying to rehabilitate Stalin. Look here, if Moscow's bakers stopped baking bread, then certainly home bakeries would sprout up everywhere, or people would begin baking their own. But no less than bread, our people need the truth about our country's past; they must know why they suffered such tragedies. Therefore I had to search for the truth, but using the methods of a craftsman.

Investigator: You wrote more than one thousand pages when everything that was to be said on the cult of personality was already published in the Central Committee's resolution of June 30, 1956.

Roy Medvedev: Yes, but the chief architect of that resolution was Molotov, who's been thrown out of the party because of the crimes he committed during the years when the Stalin cult prevailed. Of the other members of the Central Committee Presidium who approved that resolution, some have been expelled from the party, and five, including Khrushchev, have been ousted from the Presidium. So how can you treat a document like that as exhaustive? Anyway, no document is ever exhaustive, and in historical research, there's no such thing as definitive truth.

Investigator: You say that you feel no sympathy for Stalin. But historians must be objective, they can't give way to their private sentiments. Your book is too subjective.

Roy Medvedev: All historians are subjective in their evaluations. When you write about such terrible crimes committed so recently, you can't suppress your feelings. My father, remember, was one of the victims, and so were many persons dear to me.

Investigator: You not only don't agree with the most objective evaluations of Stalin in the Central Committee's resolution, but you expound your own ideas and disparage the committee's decisions.

Roy Medvedev: Yes indeed, I expound my own ideas, and I disparage the decisions adopted by the Central Committee in 1956 because they're inadequate. And why shouldn't I? The magazine *Kommunist* has published any number of articles that actually take the party to task for the decisions it approved at the Twentieth Congress and, more emphatically, at the Twenty-Second Congress, and propagate opinions on Stalin that repudiate the views of the party's highest tribunal. Why haven't you, as responsible members of the party, ever called the authors to account? And what about Kochetov's [neo-Stalinist] novel *But What Is It You Want?* Why hasn't anyone called Kochetov to account? And the same thing goes for the [pro-Stalin] poetry of Chuyev, Firsov, and S. V. Smirnov, who are also members of the party. Sergei I. Murashov, who is head of the social sciences department in the Ministry of Higher Education, has also written a history of the Soviet Communist Party, but it departs so much from the officially approved line and contains such gross [neo-Stalinist] falsifications that even the Politburo denounced it. But his book is still being sold, with 65,000 copies in circulation, and students in any number of higher educational institutions are using it to study history. Why are these writers allowed to express their ideas while I am not?

Investigator: In our archives we keep all the articles published by the bourgeois press on the Nekrich case.* If you read them you'll see who took up Nekrich's defense: for the most part our enemies. You've published your book abroad, and our enemies have shown considerable interest in what you've written.

Roy Medvedev: And haven't our enemies shown any interest in Kochetov's novel? That book was a revelation to them, but their reaction to it shouldn't surprise us. They always exploit our errors . . . it would be surprising if they didn't in the case of an error like expelling Nekrich from the party for telling the truth in his book . . . or, to be exact, the partial truth . . . about Stalinism. It wasn't Nekrich who gave them the opportunity to spread propaganda against us but the men who expelled him. In any case, in the West we don't have only enemies: everyone is interested in what's happened and what's happening in the Soviet Union. Not long ago an article of mine was published in the West, but the bourgeois press also published Brezhnev's speeches, and with comments. What's strange about that?

Investigator: Don't you think that Stalin is being damned mainly by people who feel a personal grudge against him?

Roy Medvedev: Quite possibly the resentful are more exasperated than others, but then, millions of people feel resentment toward Stalin. And why shouldn't we acknowledge their right to say what they think?

* The Nekrich case—Aleksandr Nekrich, a Soviet historian, had a book published officially in Moscow in 1966, documenting and discussing Stalin's failure to prepare the country for an attack from Germany. A controversial discussion of the book was held at the party's Institute of Marxism-Leninism and subsequently, in 1967, Nekrich was expelled from the party and the book withdrawn; he left the USSR in 1976 and now lives and works as a historian in the Boston area.

And vice versa, why should we encourage authors like Kochetov and Murashov, whose books offend the memory of all those victims who died while the cult of Stalin prevailed and of those who escaped death by mere chance . . . and the relatives of victims who suffered under his despotism?

Investigator: I'm a historian too, by training, and I can say only that the sources of your book are pretty weak.

Roy Medvedev: I agree. But if I'd had access to the archives of the Central Committee and the NKVD, to those of Stalin and his closest collaborators, and to those of the USSR's attorney general, my sources would have been more solid. But even so, do you suppose that I would have arrived at different conclusions about the crimes of Stalin and Stalinism? My job was to collect accounts and testimonies from people who were persecuted under Stalin's terror, who languished in his prison camps. Many of them have already departed this world, and within a decade many others will probably join them. These testimonies you won't find in any archives; and as for what's filed away in them, let's leave that to other historians sometime in the future.

Investigator: What's your opinion of *One Day in the Life of Ivan Denisovich?*

Roy Medvedev: That novel passed the scrutiny of the Central Committee, which authorized it for publication. I agree completely with Tvardovsky that it's an important book.

Investigator: I read two or three pages of it, but I couldn't go any further. Isn't it possible that many of the repressions you authors write about could have been deserved?

Roy Medvedev: Here *you're* in disagreement with the party's decision, not I.

These are only a few excerpts from my conversations with the party's investigators, which dragged on for hours and whole days. The result was a new report on my book, read during a meeting of the party's Control Commission, with Arvid Pelshe, a member of the Politburo, presiding. Here no one behaved discourteously, the general tone wasn't boorish as it had been at the local and city committee hearings, but the outcome was the same: I was still expelled from the party.

PO What were the consequences? Did you lose your job?

RM I was working at the Institute of Professional Education at the Academy of Pedagogical Sciences, doing research in vocational training in the upper grades in secondary schools. It's a subject

32

that caught my attention back in the '50s when I was teaching; I was also the principal of my school. In 1959 I submitted my doctoral thesis on this subject and later wrote two books on it.

After they stripped me of my party membership, I continued to work quietly at the institute; no one thought of firing me. A member of the staff of a scientific institute can be dismissed only by a vote of the institute's academic council. In the case of researchers with a certain seniority, the council pronounces its verdict every five years—and it's final. You can't appeal it to the unions or the courts, even though they have a good deal to say about who's to be fired and who isn't. So a ruling in my favor could have been expected—unless the local party committee was very insistent.

However, things took an altogether different turn. In October 1971 I resigned. My books *Let History Judge* and *A Question of Madness* were due to come out in November–December. At that time, the police made their first search of my apartment, and I thought it might be wise if I left Moscow for a while. Even though the police were shadowing me, I managed to slip out of the city and go to stay with friends in the Caucasus. No one knew where I was, not my wife, my brother, or the KGB. You know, if someone wants to vanish in the USSR, he can do it without a soul knowing where to find him . . . except the friends he stays with. Four months later I returned to Moscow; the books were out by then, and there wasn't anything anyone could do about them. I had no new summons, not even as a pretext to justify the house search.

Since then I've been unemployed, so I work independently at the library or at home. I had long dreamed of working and living in total freedom from constraining assignments, and for the past six years I've been doing exactly that.

PO I'd like to talk about the "Sakharov case," which seems to be quite different from yours. In the past few years the party apparatus has asked the Academy of Sciences twice to discipline him, but both times only about seventy members out of seven hundred obliged. Does that imply something of a conflict between the Academy and the government?

33

RM   Not at all. The Academy isn't opposed to the government. In point of fact, the Academy has disciplined Sakharov on two occasions, and the press has published accusatory declarations against him, signed by dozens of academicians. And I'm sure that hundreds more would have signed if the party had insisted. But it's one thing to sign a denunciation of Sakharov and another to expel him from the Academy and deny him his title as academician. As far as I know, nothing of the sort has ever been tried. Probably the academicians were polled to sound out their attitudes. You see, before a man can be accepted as a member of the Academy or expelled from it, the statutes require a secret ballot and a two-thirds majority in both cases. In 1973, the previous president of the Academy, Mstislav Keldysh, warned the party apparatus that he couldn't guarantee a favorable outcome if the issue of Sakharov's removal were put to a secret vote for the simple reason that people say one thing publicly but do the opposite in a secret ballot.

PO   In other words, when circumstances permit, they will resist the government's arbitrary demands. And that's what the Academy does when it can.

RM   The system of secret balloting remains an important democratic procedure which can sometimes impose limits on arbitrary power. The Academy has given the government a few surprises by rejecting various candidates backed by the party apparatus. To give you an example: Sergei P. Trapeznikov, chief of the Central Committee's department of science and a known Stalinist, was blackballed twice, but he made it on the last vote.
     On the whole, however, I wouldn't say that there's any real conflict between the Academy and the government.

PO   Well, excluding such a possibility, do you see the Academy as a pressure group with enough clout to influence the state within its own sphere?

RM   Yes, it can pressure the government within certain limits because it enjoys relative independence . . . but that independence is so restricted that you can't call the Academy a pressure group in the

34

sense you give to the term. Its funds come from the state budget, and the party organs must give their prior approval to all the most important appointments, such as who the directors will be. Within the Academy you have a rather powerful party organization, which has more to say about the selection of delegates to scientific conferences than the president of the Academy himself.

Only once has the Academy ever operated as a real pressure group in political and party affairs, and that was when it rebelled against Lysenko's faction . . . which had the government's full support under both Stalin and Khrushchev . . . for dominating practically every sector in the field of biology. The antagonism of the majority infuriated Khrushchev to such a pitch that at one point he threatened to close down the Academy altogether and replace it with a state committee for the sciences. But in practically all other instances, the Academy has upheld party policies; it's never been a bulwark of opposition.

PO Those who did not sign the denunciation of Sakharov in 1973 included ordinary members of the party and members of the Central Committee. Does that mean that they could openly state their preference for more ideological tolerance within the party?

RM If only seventy or eighty members signed the declaration, that's not because the others refused to put their names to it. The fact is simply that they were never asked to sign it. Some of the top academicians didn't reject public condemnation of Sakharov's behavior, but they didn't want their names on the document to compromise their reputations . . . abroad more than in the USSR. They're men who often travel to foreign countries and maintain contacts with foreign scientists. Pyotr Kapitsa backed out because, as he explained, he knew Sakharov personally and didn't need to notify him of his disapproval through the press. Others signed only under pressure. I'm told that in 1973 Aleksandrov, now president of the Academy, spoke out against expelling Sakharov at a meeting of the Academy, and again at a party session.

But I repeat: we mustn't pounce on this incident to exaggerate the Academy's position as a potential pressure group in the opposition. In the USSR, a scientist must make compromises and public displays of his patriotism, but his career is a long and complicated one, so that by the time he achieves the title of academician, often at an advanced age, he confines himself to his work and avoids political affairs. A lot of Academy members are as apolitical as other people.

4

The Citizen
and the State

PO   I'd like to talk about the Soviet man in the street. What legal
course does he have for expressing his dissatisfaction and bringing
his complaints to the attention of the authorities?

RM   First, we mustn't exaggerate the extent of his disaffection. The
overwhelming majority of the population unquestionably sanction
the government's power and show no particular wish to have a
run-in with the authorities by voicing grievances. But if an individual disagrees vehemently on some issue or other, he doesn't have
much choice of means to express himself.

    We don't have an independent press or independent publishers.
The major Soviet newspapers never run letters from readers who
write in about political matters they don't like, not to mention
complaints about minor or isolated inconveniences. The USSR has
never taken a serious poll of public opinion, particularly on critical political issues, and elections are useless to the dissenter because only one candidate runs on any ticket, whether for the soviets on the local or higher level.

    Nevertheless, in our country as elsewhere, there are ways in which people can make their objections known, but many of them are risky. One of the simplest is to refuse to vote; a man just stays away from the polls. In the most clamorous, of course, he renounces his citizenship and applies for an exit visa.

PO It seems that the Soviet citizen never knows exactly what he can and cannot do. I mean, there are no "legal guarantees" in the Soviet Union . . .

RM It's not easy to fix the limits . . . I don't mean imaginary limits . . . of tolerated protest. There are no fixed limits; they change from time to time and from sector to sector of political life. They're wider in the area of economics, industry, and agriculture than they are in foreign policy, for example. It's easier to criticize a minister or, in fact, the whole Council of Ministers than a secretary of the Soviet Communist Party or the Politburo. And it's still easier to lambaste the manager of the shop on the corner or the neighborhood housing agency for any shortcomings.

In Stalin's time, any protest with the faintest hint of political implications meant immediate arrest. That was the rule. But then, the limits of tolerable protest, even with political overtones, relaxed considerably. Yet almost all citizens speak their minds with great caution. They've learned their lesson from experience.

In the past, there were cases of persons sentenced to harsh punishment for complaints they'd made ten or fifteen years before. In the middle '30s, almost all of Stalin's previous opponents, who subsequently avowed their "unlimited devotion" to him, were arrested and liquidated in jails and prison camps. I know of men who were called to justice at the end of the '40s and early '50s because back in 1926–27, as members of the Komsomol they had voted with the opposition against party programs or simply abstained. The minutes of the meetings when the voting was held were dug up in the archives and handed over to the security services.

This explains what happened after the Twentieth and Twenty-Second Congresses: when people, especially writers, historians, and scientists, were finally permitted to air their grievances and

honest opinions, most intellectuals passed up the opportunity.
They were afraid that the new freedom might be rescinded and
they'd have to account for what they said and wrote. But, in fact,
things did change for them.

I must say that today the Soviet citizen is allowed more latitude
to state his grievances than he is inclined to utilize. This applies
not only to his disapproval of "grand policy" but also to the administration of some project or some government agency. Even
within today's looser strictures, people are more submissive than
they need be.

PO   What's known as the "rule of predictable reactions" seems to fall
neatly into the Soviet pattern. The phrase refers to the foregone
resignation of a political system's subjects to the power of their
bosses even when that power isn't exercised in any way.

RM   Your theory is correct, although it applies only to certain relatively
tranquil periods in the life of a society. When a country is gripped
by a national crisis that threatens to precipitate a revolution, to
use Marxist terminology, you will see situations cropping up that
negate the theory of predictable reactions. A climate is created in
which, as Lenin said, the masses no longer want to live as they
have been living, and the government is no longer able to go on
ruling as it has been ruling until that moment. At other times, however, the majority of the population will toe the line just as the
ruling power wants and expects, particularly when it's an oligarchy
as strong as the Soviet government.

PO   In essence you're saying that the people's resignation leads to the
transmutation of coercive power into consensual power, with the
result that the regime doesn't need to impose its decision. Is that
right?

RM   Yes. Soviet citizens are only dimly aware of their political and civil
rights. The government knows that, therefore it doesn't demand
any sincere consensus from them. The men in power are satisfied
with nothing more than their silence and passivity, especially in
regard to government actions that, by their very nature, couldn't

be anything but unpopular. To take one example, when Khrushchev abruptly abolished payment of premiums on government bonds and announced that they would come due only after twenty years, he knew very well that the bondholders wouldn't be happy about it; but he was sure, too, that they would accept his edict without a murmur. And when the government decrees shorter holidays, no one likes it but everyone abides by it. It's the same when the cost of consumer goods goes up, which does happen in the Soviet Union, although not so much as in the West. In such cases as these, you might have a spontaneous public outcry, but that would be a rare and unexpected exception.

Also, we have scant assurance of our political and civil rights because we have no efficient mechanism to defend them. When a citizen's rights are violated, he will petition the appeal boards or write letters to the editor or to the Central Committee, but seldom will he get any satisfaction. Most often he doesn't have the right to go to court if he's involved in a dispute with a state organization or a party organ, which has more influence and power. I, for instance, couldn't appeal to a court of law in my dispute with my local party committee or the city committee.

What I'm saying here applies mainly to political and civil rights. Where economic and social rights are involved, the story is quite different.

PO   In what way?

RM   The Soviet citizen knows that he is fully entitled to such rights as employment, education, welfare assistance, and free medical care. If he is denied these rights, he'll fight for them with tenacity, sometimes rounding up collective support from his friends and neighbors. Usually he wins. He knows that he has the right to see a doctor any time he wants or to have the doctor make a house call. He knows that his children have the right to be educated in a free school. These services are all gratis. He's sure of his right to work and he demands that a job be provided.

To dismiss the Soviet citizen as a passive, apolitical human being is entirely erroneous. When he has no doubts about what is due him by law, he will act with forthright courage and energy. For one thing, he's accustomed to efficient public transportation that runs on time. Once when the traffic on the Prospekt Mira (the Avenue of Peace, in Moscow) was blocked for some reason and crowds of people collected at the bus stops, they suddenly swarmed across that wide boulevard and stopped every vehicle that came along. When the traffic police asked them to clear the way, they demanded that the bus service be resumed immediately so that they could go home. The militia had no choice but to oblige them and, after only a few minutes, dozens of emergency buses arrived on the scene. This incident illustrates what I'm saying: that when Soviet citizens are sure of their rights, they'll often take tough action to make sure they get them.

PO This brings us to another important "knotty question." In substance, the system guarantees the people all rights, including political and civil, but sometimes it subordinates political rights, depending upon prevailing circumstances and what the government considers convenient and within permissible limits. In that context, the Soviet Constitution provides that some rights can be granted only when they strengthen socialism, build Communism, and advance the welfare of the workers. But who decides whether a given right will strengthen socialism, build Communism, and benefit the worker? And how is that decision arrived at?

RM Your question touches on one of the weakest points in our legislation and in the Soviet way of life. The Soviet Constitution guarantees freedom of speech, freedom of the press, assembly, and public demonstrations, but only insofar as these freedoms operate "in the interests of the workers and with the aim of strengthening socialism." But who decides what's in the interest of the workers and what isn't?

At the Sixteenth Congress of the Soviet trade unions at the end of March 1977, Brezhnev had this to say about the dissidents:

In our country it is not forbidden "to think differently" from the majority, to appraise critically various aspects of public life. We regard the comrades who come out with substantiated criticism, who

41

strive to improve matters, as conscientious critics, and we are grateful to them. Those who criticize erroneously we regard as people who err. It is quite another matter if a few individuals who have broken away from our society actively come out against the socialist system, embark on the road of anti-Soviet activity, violate laws and, finding no support inside their own country, turn for support abroad, to imperialist subversive centers—propaganda and intelligence centers. Our people demand that such—if you will excuse the expression—activists be treated as opponents of socialism, as persons acting against their own motherland, as accomplices, if not actual agents, of imperialism. Quite naturally, we have taken and will continue to take against them measures envisaged by our law.*

Perhaps for the first time, this speech attempts to separate the heterodox into various categories. But in each case the question arises, who is going to make the distinction between those "with substantiated criticism" and those "who err"? And by what criteria? Marxism establishes a precise principle, in my view absolutely correct, which states that the criterion of truth lies in practical activity. This means that only time and life itself can determine which observations are correct and which are not. Truth can be verified only by human and social praxis. But another principle emerged from Brezhnev's speech: that only the party and its institutions can pronounce the final verdict on what is right and what is wrong. But where is the guarantee that their judgments are correct? Not long ago it was fashionable to say that only the individual can be wrong, the party never. Now we know from history that individual party leaders and the party itself have been wrong many times, and some of their mistakes have persisted for years, for decades, whereas persons thought for years to be "in error" or even downright "enemies of the people" have subsequently been vindicated entirely by the party itself.

Another point in Brezhnev's speech isn't altogether clear: what attitude should the state take toward a third category of the heterodox? Certainly it's understandable that every state will persecute those who agitate against it or who turn to foreign secret services for help. But why may citizens in a socialist society de-

* The English wording is from *Reprints from the Soviet Press*, April 30, 1977, pp. 22–23.

nounce only certain aspects of public life? What if they disapprove
of socialism altogether or, as we say today, this or that model of a
socialist society? Why can't they enjoy the elementary rights of any
democracy, freedom of speech, of opinion, of the press? Is it because in our country the ideological struggle must be fought not
through words and concepts but through repression? We've always
known that repression can silence people but it can't change their
opinions: to the contrary, it will only swell the ranks of those
"who err." The Communist parties in Western Europe don't attack isolated apsects of capitalism but capitalism as a whole. Then
why shouldn't the USSR be a more democratic state in the formal
sense than Italy or France or England?

In spite of our sixty years of experience with Soviet power,
marked by a wealth of successes as well as serious reverses, the notion that the Central Committee and the Politburo are infallible
stubbornly persists in the minds of the Soviet people. But this ob-
session is no less questionable than the infallibility of the Pope,
even if the Pope is consecrated by a Concilium.

PO   The Soviet leaders often admit their past mistakes and promise not
to make any more in the future, yet they're apparently incapable
of investing the present with democracy. The past must have been
more democratic, and the future will be too, but for the present,
democratic policies don't exist. Why is that?

RM   Even if we accept your generalizations, you must still agree that on
the whole it is far easier to avoid error when looking back historically than it is when involved in current political activity, when
decisions have to be made on the spur of the moment and in highly
complex circumstances. But I wouldn't say that every political
decision taken by the Soviet government is necessarily wrong and
every one taken by a democratic government necessarily right.
Even after democratic debates, which allow the opposition to speak
up, many governments still go astray. Of course, in an authoritarian system the possible margin of error is greater because it
leaves no room for a deeper probing of the issue at hand. But
hasn't the United States government committed any number of

43

mistakes in the past ten years? And didn't President Carter bungle a whole series of issues within the first hundred days of his presidency, which the Western press properly denounced?

What I'm saying is that philosophy . . . or that part of it which deals with forecasting the future . . . goes astray perhaps no less than politics. We've made our share of blunders. Still you can't deny that Soviet society is advancing, that it's pretty solid, which is more than you can say about many capitalist countries. Once someone asked a famous economist, "In your opinion, which society is more effective, capitalist or socialist?" and he answered with a wink, "Socialist, of course, because if the capitalist world made as many mistakes as our government does in the area of economics, it would have collapsed by now, while our socialist world still stands on its feet and goes on developing."

PO   Regional nationalism is another source of dissent. The Constitution nominally allows the separate republics to secede if they want, yet if anyone speaks openly about this provision, he'll land in the prisoners' dock because Article 70 of the penal code forbids any "agitation or propaganda intended to subvert or weaken Soviet power." How, then, does the so-called "protest of the nationalities" express itself?

RM   I wouldn't generalize about unrest among the non-Russian nationalities. Of course, some of our nationalities are discontented with their lot, primarily the Crimean Tatars, who are still not allowed to return to their home territory and have no national autonomy.* And the Volga Germans, who've never regained their autonomy either, have good reason to be restive.† Most Jews are distressed

---

* Descendants of the Mongol-Tatar conquerors who established a state in the Crimea in the fifteenth century. Stalin had the entire population deported to Siberia and Central Asia in May 1944 on the absurd grounds that every Crimean Tatar—man, woman, and child—had collaborated with the Nazi occupation. In 1967 a Supreme Soviet decree withdrew the wholesale charge of treason but denied the Tatars' right to return to the Crimea. A protest movement for the right to return arose and has continued ever since.

† The Volga Germans were descendants of German settlers invited by the tsar in the eighteenth century; the Stalin regime deported them wholesale from the Volga region to Siberia and Kazakhstan after the German invasion in 1941. Like the Crimean Tatars, they have not been allowed to return to their former lands or to have their own republic (with autonomous status inside the RSFSR) restored.

44

because of the discrimination against them, and they've been emigrating *en masse* from the USSR. But the other nationalities . . . yes, they have their problems to contend with, but they don't stage any mass protests.

It's not true to say that anyone who talks openly about the republics' right to secede will be punished according to the strictures of the penal code. There's no clause in any code that calls for any such persecution. Those who are punished are usually militants actually working for their republic's secession from the USSR or trying to organize something like independent nationalist parties, or talking in public about Russia's exploitation of the republics, and so on. In such cases, as far as I know, there's no repression on a mass scale, it's rather selective. Yes, men like Moroz, Chornovil, and Svitychny—all Ukrainians—are serving time in prison camps,* but other protesters have been subjected only to administrative measures and other lesser forms of pressure. Certainly such treatment is illegal. Since the Constitution recognizes the right of a republic to secede, any propaganda in favor of separatism shouldn't be a pretext for punishment in any form.

Incidentally, most Soviet citizens accused of nationalism are penalized not under Article 70 but Article 74, which refers to encouraging discrimination and inciting national or racial animosity. Here let me remind you that while the Constitution allows for secession, it doesn't clarify how this right can be implemented or guaranteed; no separatist mechanism has ever been legalized or even devised.

PO I agree that "national dissent," like dissent in general, is not a mass phenomenon in the USSR. But the fact remains that your country is a crucible of nationalities, often divided by rivalries and ancient rancors. Can we talk about that briefly?

RM This is a very complicated question. There's no single explana-

---

*In May 1979 Valentyn Moroz was released and flown to the United States, along with Aleksandr Ginzburg and three other prominent Soviet political prisoners, in a much publicized "exchange" for two Soviet government personnel who had been convicted of espionage in a U.S. court. Moroz had been sentenced to nine years imprisonment and five years internal exile in November 1970. Chornovil and Svitlychny are serving terms of internal exile, after completing long prison sentences.

tion—an adequate reply would require a whole volume. You see, national problems vary from region to region, and those whom we might term "local nationalists" want solutions to a wide range of regional problems. To begin with, the West exaggerates the importance of our nationalist movements. The Soviet authorities aren't misrepresenting the facts when they say that the national components of the old tsarist Russian empire . . . the framework of the present Soviet state . . . have experienced rapid change in both national-cultural and economic structures, and that they have profited enormously from the October revolution. In the past, the authorities put much effort into solving all kinds of regional issues; therefore I don't believe there's any danger of the USSR breaking up. All the same, a great many problems still persist.

Let me say that while most of the demands put forth by the national movements are justified and need solutions, many others are downright unrealistic—understandable, but impossible to meet within the context of a multinational state like the USSR.

PO For example?

RM For one thing, you can't do without the Russian language . . . the language not only of the Russians but also of the state . . . which enables the different nationalities to communicate with one another. At one point, the Ukrainians insisted on using only their own tongue for business and all official correspondence; they actually removed all typewriters with Russian characters from their business offices and government ministries. When a minister sent a letter in Ukrainian to Moscow, there was always someone who could make it out. But in Tajikistan or Armenia they couldn't understand letters from the Ukraine. So they began to reply in Tajik or Armenian. During a national scientific conference, the Ukrainian delegates spoke in Ukrainian, the Georgians read their papers in Georgian, and so on. Naturally, before long everyone had to revert to Russian.

Most scientific and literary works are published in Russian in all the republics. A book on mathematics or philosophy published in Georgian, say, would have no circulation outside Georgia. Most

Ukrainian families prefer to send their children to Russian schools, as do parents even in the small autonomous republics. Newspapers printed in regional languages or television and radio programs broadcast in them cannot compete with those in Russian.

This is an inevitable process, difficult to arrest or to resolve in a short time. In the Soviet Union, the centripetal forces are more powerful than the centrifugal.

PO The rise of the colonial empires dominated by the Western nations came after those nations achieved their territorial unity. Then, to acquire their colonies, they had to cross the sea. From the very outset, their conquest of alien territories and the races that inhabited them was tantamount to sheer plunder. But the Russian empire took shape territorially and chronologically with the foundation of the Russian national state. Tsarist Russia wasn't obliged to cross the sea to become a colonial power; therefore it never clearly assumed the same aggressive face as the West did.

A young Ukrainian nationalist once said to me, "The fate of the Algerians aroused the sympathy of the whole world, but no one weeps for the fate of the Soviet nationalities. . . ." I'd like to know what you think about this?

RM It's true that the Russian empire didn't take form as the Western colonial powers did. That's why the most serious experts today never talk about Russian colonialism. But Western propaganda often speaks of "Russian imperialism" and refers to the non-Russian republics in the USSR as Russian colonies. Soviet propaganda also casts the national entities in the image of colonies, but only when it refers to tsarist Russia. Indeed, we can't deny that Russia's behavior toward the territories it assimilated was much the same as the Western powers' treatment of their colonies. But since the revolution, you can't say that the USSR is a colonial empire or that its republics are colonies.

Certainly, remnants of what Lenin called great power chauvinism still survive. The USSR today is not so much a federation as a unitary state, since the union republics enjoy only a negligible degree of independence; and there's not much independence to

47

talk about when the dominant factor in all the republics is the Soviet Communist Party, with its totally unified organizational structure. Nevertheless, I'm sure that if the government proclaimed a referendum in the union republics, the majority of the people would vote to remain in the USSR.

The Western nations conquered territories in Asia and Africa to appropriate their natural wealth, particularly raw materials, and utilized them primarily to satisfy their domestic needs. In our case, after the October revolution . . . and this is an irreversible process . . . our national entities developed economically and culturally much faster than the colonies of the West . . . and with visible results. But while Russian culture predominates throughout the USSR simply because the Russian population is the largest and Russian is the official national language, the opposite is true of Russia's material situation. In regions in the heart of Russia, such as Vologda, Arkhangelsk, Leningrad, Kalinin, Smolensk, Vladimir, the standard of living is notably lower than in Georgia, Armenia, Azerbaijan, Moldavia, the Baltic republics, Central Asia , and the Ukraine. I'd say that after the revolution, Russia conferred greater cultural and economic benefits on the other nationalities than it received in return. Moscow is the exception, of course; its standard of living is much higher than that in the other Russian cities.

PO If the Russian Republic doesn't exploit the other republics, as the Western nations did their colonies, it still controls them politically through its centralized economic planning. It doesn't allow them to evolve their own economies as they'd like to do, and therefore deprives them of any real autonomy in decision-making. What's your opinion?

RM If our republics have no real political or economic autonomy, that's not because Russia . . . that is, the RSFSR, . . . controls them. The Russian Republic has even less autonomy. Control lies in the hands of such central seats of power as the Central Committee of the CPSU—and according to the Constitution, the CPSU stands over and above all the republics, including the Russian.

48

In countries like the Soviet Union, economic planning embraces the interests of the entire state and provides for a division of labor calculated on a statewide basis. It wouldn't make much sense to convert the cotton plantations of Uzbekistan into wheat fields or Georgia's tea plantations, vineyards, and market gardens, which supply the entire domestic market with their produce, to potato cultivation. Nor would it be logical to build a steel mill in Georgia to produce steel only for Georgia.

You have analogous processes of economic integration in Western Europe, which raise the question of political integration and consequently exacerbate every kind of national problem.

PO That's right. I've noticed, however, that the Russians harbor a certain animosity toward the Georgians, for example, and all the other nationalities whose standard of living is higher than theirs. And another thing: I have the impression that as the process of modernization advances in the different national republics, they intensify their demands for more autonomy. In other words, could the same thing happen in the USSR, perhaps to a lesser degree, that has occurred in the West . . . I mean, could a new ruling class in your "colonies" set off an anti-colonial revolt against the Russians?

RM Marx said that colonialism doesn't mean only the plundering of the colonies but also, in the long run, their modernization because colonialism uproots the colonies' ancient feudal way of life and initiates a process of development, which sooner or later brings an end to the colonial system. The metamorphosis of the USSR's nationalities came about altogether differently. All the same, as I see it, their development isn't increasing the centrifugal forces in the country, but rather is reducing them. Moreover, we see that ancient antagonisms pitting one region against another are disappearing, and the separate nationalities are drawing closer together.

It would be wrong to think that the [official] statements about the growing friendship among the peoples of the USSR are just words. Still, it is true that strong anti-Russian feelings persist in some republics, just as the inhabitants in some parts of Russia still

49

distrust and dislike the people of other Soviet nationalities. I've often encountered such hostilities in the popular vacation resorts of the Northern Caucasus, places like Kislovodsk, Piatigorsk, Zheleznovodsk, and Yessentuki, where hundreds of thousands of people come from all over Russia and Transcaucasia to spend their summer holidays. Sometimes their resentment has to do with material imbalances. Families from Kalinin, Tula, or Novgorod are usually less well off than families from Baku and Tbilisi. To put it briefly, I don't believe, as many Westerners do, that our national problems can produce any disruptive effect on the Soviet system, now or in the future.

PO   At this point, is it possible to estimate how many active dissidents there are in the USSR?

RM   Only a few dissidents are saying what they think or making adverse comments in public on any government action, which doesn't necessarily imply an open protest against the regime. Their number varies from time to time: in 1967–68 a few thousand, at the beginning of the '60s a few hundred, now a few dozen. Of course, if you include those in confinement, again they would count in the hundreds or two to four thousand.

Unfortunately, once they've been released, most dissidents don't rejoin the movement; either they abandon it or they emigrate. Sinyavsky and Daniel are typical examples. Sinyavsky left the country and now lives in France. Daniel is still with us in the Soviet Union, but he quit the movement.* Incidentally, let me point out that almost every dissident has his own "nucleus" of friends and followers who give him their sympathy and help even if he doesn't issue statements.

PO   So that, for better or worse, the system enjoys an almost unanimous consensus . . .

---

* Since the time of this interview Daniel did act in defense of his friend and former prison-camp comrade Aleksandr Ginzburg. Daniel spoke at a Moscow press conference for foreign journalists on February 3, 1978, the anniversary of Ginzburg's arrest (as reported by The Chronicle of Current Events, No. 49, May 1978).

RM Without opinion polls, which don't exist in the Soviet Union, it's difficult to arrive at any quantitative evaluation. And then, we must explain exactly what we mean by the word "system." If we refer not to a well-defined government but rather to socialism as a social system, then certainly today it claims the consensus of practically the entire population. Therefore it's no use hoping for a change; that would be about as unrealistic as the idea of turning present-day Europe back to the eighteenth century. The system can only be improved . . . just as it can also be worsened by a bad government. Within this consensus there can be a certain amount of dissatisfaction with particular aspects of the system, such as waste and disorganization, rampant corruption, and a shortage of consumer goods. Sometimes the people make known their disappointment in one regime or another. Khrushchev, for example, lost the good will of the majority during the last years he headed the government. But people recognize the difference between individual leaders and the system as a whole.

But if by the term "system" we mean not socialism but domination by the party, then I will say that beyond all doubt the vast majority of the population endorses the Soviet Communist Party. Naturally the millions of party and state functionaries, the managers, and most of the intellectuals in government service are anxious to preserve the system; it makes life easier. A more pluralistic order would create too many headaches for them. Then, don't forget too, that if most people approve of Soviet Communism, at least passively, they've never lived under any other system.

So you see, our present form of government possesses such tremendous reserves that neither external pressures nor dissident agitation could, by themselves, bring about fundamental changes. Any change would require the force of these factors combined with an initiative from "above." Many dissidents and emigrants strongly contest this theory of mine, and some of them believe there's no more hope for any initiative from "above." But that's not true.

5

Thaw and
Neo-Stalinism

PO   Is it possible to establish a more or less accurate date for the incep-
     tion of the dissident movement in the USSR?

RM   If you mean the contemporary movement, it began approximately
     in the summer of 1965, following the Central Committee's Plenum
     in October 1964 when the Committee removed Khrushchev from
     office and the Stalinists raised the issue of rehabilitating Stalin. As
     yet there was no unity among Khrushchev's successors, and along
     with various intelligent reforms, such as the economic reform, the
     government passed some really senseless legislation. Khrushchev's
     fall, like the collapse of Stalin before him, precipitated a crisis in
     the authority of the Communist Party and the government which
     created a psychological dilemma that spurred various social groups
     to organize and, as we say, fed the ferment among the population.
         This unrest passed through several stages, beginning with pro-
     tests against the moves toward rehabilitating Stalin. Then in De-
     cember 1965 a demonstration against the arrest of Sinyavsky and

Daniel was held in Pushkin Square.* The trials of 1966–67
sparked still more massive protests in the form of petitions and
new demonstrations. Hundreds, even thousands, protested against
the trial of Sinyavsky and Daniel and against the trial of Galanskov, Ginzburg, and Lashkova.† *Samizdat* hit its peak. Indeed, all
the Soviet dissidents known in the West were "men of the '60s";
that's as true of those who were expatriated as of those who stayed
behind. Of course, new dissidents come forward, and sometimes
they attract a good deal of attention, as Aleksandr Zinoviev has
with his book *The Yawning Heights*, but they're more the exception than the rule.

But taking a broader view of the dissident movement, we shall
see that it has always existed and, over the years, changed only its
forms, its methods, and aims. *Samizdat* dates back much farther
than 1965. By the 1920s any number of underground manuscripts,
articles on various subjects and programs were circulating in the
country. For the most part, these items referred to internal party
disputes and were distributed among party members.

Under Stalin himself, a dissident movement existed in the most
profound secrecy, but it was a feeble one; and after the war, young
anti-Stalinists set up political clubs, but we know very little about
them because they left almost no written documents behind. Immediately after Stalin's death, a great deal of *samizdat* poetry began
to circulate. Tvardovsky's poem *Tyorkin in the Other World*, in its
first version (1954), passed from hand to hand, as did poems by
Akhmatova, Berggolts, Slutsky, Yevtushenko, and others. Then,
right after the Twenty-Second Congress, journalistic and scientific

---

* The demonstration was held on December 5, 1965—Constitution Day, so called because
the Soviet constitution then in effect had been adopted on December 5, 1936. The demon-
strators called for an open trial for Sinyavsky and Daniel (arrested in September 1965) and
for "respect for the constitution." It became a central theme of the movement that the rights
granted in the Constitution should be honored in practice. Since 1965, demonstrations by
human-rights activists in the USSR have been held every year on Constitution Day.

† The trial of Yuri Galanskov, Aleksandr Ginzburg, Vera Lashkova, and Aleksei Dobrovolsky (who turned against his fellow dissidents and testified for the prosecution) was held in
Moscow in January 1968. They were persecuted for having produced *samizdat* works, especially a "White Book" with the trial transcript of the Sinyavsky-Daniel case as well as the texts
of many protest statements and other documents in that case.

works began to circulate in *samizdat*. One of the first scientific pieces, an essay entitled "Biological Science and the Personality Cult,"* written by my brother Zhores, contributed largely to the rapid downfall of Lysenko and his clique. In 1964 Eugenia Ginzburg's *Journey Into the Whirlwind* was widely circulated in manuscript, as were memoirs by Olitskaya Nadezhda [a surviving member of the old SR Party (Socialist Revolutionaries)], Mandelstam, and others.

It appears that the dissident movement which took form in 1965 is now dying out, but dissent is turning up today in new guises. The very fact that dissidents and dissent exist is a symptom of a live, vital society. There are reasons for discontent in every country. On the other hand, the government's persistent efforts to suppress all expressions of opposition reveal that there is a malady in our society. But our leaders try to cover it up instead of trying to cure it.

PO   Would you identify the opposition before 1965 as mainly intra-party dissension while the opposition after 1965 extended beyond the party?

RM   The internecine strife among the party figures who led the revolution lasted only until the end of the '20s. In the higher echelons, of course, it continued even after all the known factions had been liquidated. The infighting deteriorated into a virulent purge, and tens of thousands of party cadres were eliminated along with hundreds of thousands of rank-and-file party members. Some of them might have become dissenters in the camps, but there any open show of heresy meant instant death. Because Stalin had consolidated his power by the '40s, the feuds in the top party echelons resembled palace intrigue. But I wouldn't say that those of Stalin's comrades and collaborators who wrangled among themselves were actually dissidents any more than the party officials were who sometimes bridled at Khrushchev's leadership when he stood at the helm.

* Published in English as *The Rise and Fall of T. D. Lysenko* (New York: Columbia University Press, 1969).

55

Apart from this infighting, during the '20s there was certainly strife outside the party. Conspiratorial nuclei opposed to the party power were formed, in strictest secrecy; they were the leftover rear guard of the anti-Communist and anti-Soviet forces defeated in the civil war of 1917–22. The nature of these movements varied, but those who took part in them were considered counter-revolutionaries. As they were exposed one by one, the regime either liquidated them or condemned them to life imprisonment.

But the dissidents who emerged on the political scene in 1965 were by no means counter-revolutionaries. Usually they were intellectuals or young people raised and educated under the Soviet system, who demanded that the regime respect Soviet law and the party measures enacted at the Twentieth and Twenty-Second Congresses. Then too, various groups, unquestionably anti-Soviet, came to light, but here again, they were organized by persons who had grown up under Soviet power; no one had deprived them of their privileges or taken away their private property, nor did they come under the heading of "hostile classes." And they didn't constitute a new party because they subscribed to a wide spectrum of political orientations.

That was a groundswell of defiant opinion, often of social thinking and civic consciousness. Two events brought it about: one, for the first time the public learned about the terrible crimes committed in the '30s and '40s; and two, during the first half of the '60s, the government allowed a certain measure of liberalization, a thaw. The old methods of persecuting the heterodox were compromised by then, and new ones hadn't yet been invented.

PO   About the origins of dissent . . . Westerners often confuse cause with effect. They tend to associate the beginnings and rise of dissent with outbreaks of intensive repression, whereas, if I understand you correctly, the dissidents showed themselves only when the waves of repression subsided . . . that is, with Khrushchev's anti-Stalin campaign and the Twentieth Congress.

RM   That's right. But repression, too, has had a strong influence on the spread of the dissident movement. In fact, it reached its maximum expansion when, after de-Stalinization, the partial thaw, and mass

56

rehabilitation, the government tried to restore Stalin's prestige, and renewed its persecutions in the form of semi-secret court trials. That induced the reaction we later called "dissent."

In the West, you rightly ascribe a special significance to the Twentieth Congress, but for the development of public opinion in the Soviet Union, the Twenty-Second Congress had far greater importance. Khrushchev's report denouncing Stalin's crimes, which he delivered to the Twentieth Congress, was a matter of the deepest secrecy: the press was not allowed to mention it. When it was eventually read during the course of various meetings held all over the country, there was no discussion of its contents. People were astounded by the revelations, but they were still afraid—and even more afraid when, one or two months after the Twentieth Congress, they began to detect a noticeable cooling off, which began when the editorial staff of the periodical *Voprosy Istorii* was fired and other similarly ominous incidents occurred. Back in 1956, Khrushchev had praised Stalin as a great Marxist-Leninist, whose good name, he said, would never be left in "the hands of the party's enemies." The unrest that summer in Poland and Hungary and China's negative view of the Twentieth Congress thwarted any hope of liberalizing the party and the regime in general. After the Hungarian revolt in the autumn, the pressure rose in Soviet society. Stalin's corpse remained undisturbed in the mausoleum on Red Square and all the trappings of his cult were preserved. Stalingrad was still called Stalingrad; as were Stalinabad, Stalinogorsk, and Stalino, not to mention the thousands of streets, squares, business concerns, collective farms, and journals bearing his name. In 1959 the press extolled his name, and the nation celebrated his eightieth birthday.

It wasn't surprising that millions of people who had been rehabilitated and had returned to their families after the Twentieth Congress continued to fear that at any moment persecution might resume and they might be sent back to the prison camps. Only a few found the courage to write their memoirs during those years.

PO When would you say the break with the past occurred, making it impossible to take the country back to a Stalin-type regime?

57

RM Only after the Twenty-Second Congress did the Soviet people really begin to regain political consciousness. Perhaps at that
congress less was said than at the Twentieth Congress, but it was
said openly and published in the press. Not only Khrushchev but
practically all the speakers talked about Stalin's evildoing. After
the Congress, Stalin's remains were removed from the mausoleum,
his monuments vanished everywhere, and all the cities, streets,
and business firms named after him were rebaptized, except for a
few streets in Georgia [his birthplace]. The press began to publish
accounts of his victims' travails: Tukhachevsky, Bliukher, Pos-
tyshev, Kossior, Eikhe, Chubar', and hundreds of others.*

Soviet literature changed, too. After the Twentieth Congress,
books like Nikolaeva's novel *Battle Along the Way* and Dudintsev's
Not by Bread Alone were the highest expression of courage. Then,
one year after the Twenty-Second Congress, Solzhenitsyn published his novel *One Day in the Life of Ivan Denisovich*, while
other books came out, less valid artistically but no less powerful in
their impact on the reader. And the history of the Communist organizations in all the republics underwent revisions.

The top party leaders endorsed this current of opinion in favor
of de-Stalinization, many of them conforming in their behavior to
the "rule of predictable reactions" I've already mentioned. Although this interval lasted only briefly, after the October 1964 plenum [which removed Khrushchev] it was clearly no longer possible
to turn back. Hence, the dissident movement arose from the
aborted attempt to reverse the process of de-Stalinzation.

PO Previously, that is at the end of the '50s and beginning of the '60s,
you had an outbreak of nonconformism, with mostly poets in the
vanguard. Yevtushenko read his poems on Moscow's Mayakovsky
Square, and other poets everywhere, even in the remote Far East,
shared his ideas. Was it poetry, then, that caused the rupture?
And if so, why poetry?

RM There's no question that after the Twentieth Congress there arose,
if not a movement, a new attitude on the part of a certain section

* Tukhachevsky et al.—leading figures in the Soviet military and party leadership in the
1930s who, though loyal to Stalin, were nevertheless purged.

of public opinion. This new outlook was very evident in gatherings at the monument on Mayakovsky Square, when Yevtushenko and lesser-known poets read their works. On those occasions, the poems seemed extremely bold, but in content you couldn't compare them with "Stalin's Heirs" or "Babi Yar," also by Yevtushenko. You see, by its very nature, poetry expresses popular sentiments more aptly than politics can, or history, or philosophy, or even prose. That's because it's so full of meaning . . . not openly but rather through symbols and allusions, which aren't obscure in the least to the listener.

PO   For the sake of convenience, people divide the history of the dissident movement into three phases: first, the reawakening to the shortcomings of socialist realism and, consequently, the agitation for creative freedom; second, the will to know and to make known what happened under Stalin's reign, with *One Day in the Life of Ivan Denisovich* as the point of departure; and third, the explicit demand for civil rights. Do you agree with these divisions?

RM   I wouldn't say that your exegesis is historically accurate. True, literature did prevail in the first phase and supplied the premise for the civil rights movement. But in that literature, the plea for creative freedom coincided with the actual *process* of creating a given work. First, an author wrote his book, then he battled to have it published. I mean he had to fight the censors. The first and second phases are distinct by logic but not historically.

PO   Well then, let's talk about the first two phases as one. What were their most outstanding characteristics?

RM   The most outstanding was a driving will to discover the whole truth about the history of our country, especially the recent Stalin era. Following the Twenty-Second Congress, hundreds of people sat down to write about that era . . . literary works, memoirs, histories of the period . . . and a flood of books came out, naturally of greater or lesser historical and artistic value. Solzhenitsyn wasn't the first; Varlam Shalamov had written his cycle of stories on Kolyma, Eugenia Ginzburg had produced her epic work, and before that, Suren Gazaryan had begun his memoirs, *This Must*

Not Happen Again. That isn't to say that these writers were attacking socialist realism. Well, Andrei Sinyavsky did earlier, at the end of the '50s under the pseudonym of Abram Tertz, but the majority of authors and memoirists never wrote anything against either the system or the party. They believed that simply by telling the truth they were making a valid contribution toward a better socialism and fulfilling the objectives of the Twenty-Second Congress.

Although Solzhenitsyn's novel wasn't the first, it was certainly the most important *among those that were published*; it opened the way to the phenomenon that later became known—inaccurately— as the "literature of the camps." The periodicals began looking around for material of this kind. But then, in the summer of 1964, just a few months before his ouster, Khrushchev ordered a ban on all literature about the camps.

PO   The period in which writers exposed the horrors of the prison camps is marked by the publication of *One Day in the Life of Ivan Denisovich* and it involves Tvardovsky's review *Novy Mir*, which published the novel. Let me ask you: how is it that the government permitted authors to write so freely about such an evil epoch in the history of your country?

RM   Like the proceedings at the Twentieth and Twenty-Second Congresses, I don't think we should give credit to the government in general but rather to the personal initiative taken by Khrushchev and his closest collaborators. A lot of people opposed them for allowing that freedom from censorship. But Khrushchev stood by his guns. Today we know how *One Day in the Life of Ivan Denisovich* came to be published. My brother wrote a detailed account of it in his book *Ten Years After Ivan Denisovich,* and you'll find another account, even more detailed, in the book *Reply to Solzhenitsyn*, by V. Ya. Lakshin, a prominent Soviet critic and Tvardovsky's assistant on *Novy Mir.* Lakshin's book has thus far appeared only in France (1976), but the Russian text ran in the second issue of the almanac *Dvadtsaty Vek* (Twentieth Century), published in London under my direction. Strange as it may seem, the most inaccurate and subjective version of this signal episode in the history of Soviet literature was given by Solzhenitsyn himself in his book *The Oak and the Calf.*

PO After *Ivan Denisovich* came out, Tvardovsky conferred with Khrushchev about eventually abolishing censorship, on the plea that the censors of the Glavlit* were less educated than the editors of the publishing houses and literary magazines. Indeed, Tvardovsky satirizes their ignorance in one of his poems. He told Khrushchev that editors should decide for themselves what to publish. At first Khrushchev agreed, but then he backed down. This happened at the beginning of 1963. What induced him to change his mind?

RM Khrushchev had no authority to abolish censorship, and he didn't abolish it; that was a matter for the Presidium of the Central Committee. The Presidium listened to a series of proposals by Khrushchev and made no objections; it proceeded to eliminate the ministries of the different industrial sectors, replacing them with regional economic councils (*sovnarkhozy*), to divide the regional party committees into industrial and agricultural units; and it approved a whole array of similar reforms, obviously irrational, all of them canceled after Khrushchev fell. But in spite of his insistence, the Presidium refused to do away with censorship, and on several occasions, Khrushchev authorized works on his own responsibility without passing them on to the censors for scrutiny. One was Tvardovsky's poem *Tyorkin in the Other World.* Here's how it happened. After a conference of writers, with a number of foreign authurs present, Khrushchev invited the most famous of them to his villa in the South. Tvardovsky read the poem to the gathering, and Khrushchev gave him his permission to publish it. The same night Tvardovsky sent it by air mail to Khrushchev's son-in-law Adzhubei in Moscow . . . Adzhubei was then director of *Izvestia* . . . and it appeared in the paper the next day. A month later *Novy Mir* reprinted it. Using Tyorkin's adventures in the next world as a pretext and recounting his conversations with his companion-in-arms, who explains the nether regions to him,

* Glavlit—acronym for the Chief Administration for Literary Affairs and Publishing, the Soviet censorship agency which must approve all materials before official publication.

Tvardovsky made fun of the censors. Here's what Tyorkin's friend has to say about them:

Why look for them? We've plenty.
An abundance.
And what utter fools—
In the System, in the Network.

. . . .

We're conducting a planned program
Here with fools,

Studying them thoroughly,
Their nature, ways, and habits.
We've a special Administration
To direct the task.
It's busily engaged in shifting
Fools from job to job.
Sending them to lower posts,
Discovering them locally,

Moving these to here and those to there
—A solid program's all lined up.

. . . .

Naturally, there all are kinds of people.

Some you ask to move aside
But they won't retire.
These we generally make censors—
With a raise in pay.

From that job
There's nowhere further to move them. *

Someone told me that when the poem appeared in *Izvestia*, work came to a halt in the central sector of Glavlit; some of the censors went out and got drunk. Everyone assumed that censorship would pass out of existence from one day to the next, but it didn't. It was useful to Khrushchev, who was preparing to lay the foundation of his personality cult. His liberalism was sincere but inconstant, and often he smothered it in his outbursts of rage.

PO In some people's opinion, it was actually the debate on Stalin that prompted the government to stiffen its attitude. In speaking of

* The English wording is taken from the version of "Tyorkin in the Other World," published in *Khrushchev and the Arts* (Cambridge, MIT Press, 1965).

Stalin, one inevitably got around to the subject of his accomplices; some were still holding down important posts in the party and state agencies, including Khrushchev himself. That led to a discussion on the very nature of Soviet power. Khrushchev was fundamentally more liberal than Stalin but no less anti-democratic. But however liberal, his decisions, too, were arbitrary, personal, and undemocratic. I should say that the third phase in the course of dissent—the demand for political and civil rights—grew out of this contradiction.

RM In part, yes. In those years, the literature on Stalinism never posed the problem of the regime's power in direct terms; indirectly, however, it brought up questions in people's minds: How could such things have happened? Was the system somehow defective? Negative reactions to our past errors spread and intensified, and new literary works began to deprecate Khrushchev's subjective methods too, although in disguised language.

In 1954–55 "peasant literature," that is, the literature of the rural world, criticized the organizational forms in agriculture under Stalin but commented favorably on the progress then under way. But in 1962 the peasants' situation worsened again—and Stalin had nothing to do with that. In some works of this "peasant" trend you could clearly detect strong antagonism to Khrushchev's reforms, many of which did nothing to improve matters. People began to entertain doubts about the government's methods and its guarantees against arbitrary rule. Indeed, no one could go on for long discussing and condemning the Stalinist period and its crimes without stumbling into the problem of democratizing society. It's no exaggeration to say that literature went a long way toward awakening the civic consciousness of millions of people, and the most courageous of them helped to expand that awareness by raising new problems and applying new methods.

The great majority of authors and poets did not come to the defense of civil rights; they simply went on turning out their novels and poems and trying to find a publisher for them. All the same, from the very beginning, their output spurred the civil rights movement, which attracted mostly people outside the world of letters. This movement was linked with such names as Litvinov, Pavlinchuk, Grigorenko, Sakharov, Chalidze, Tszukerman, Yakir, Galanskov, Bukovsky, Bogoraz, Aleksandr Ginzburg, Tverdokhlebov, and many others—people of various orientations, different scales of values, and with different motivations drawing them to the democratic fold. But certainly they were the ones who sounded the call for what you term the third phase of the dissident movement. In a parallel phenomenon, popular sentiment began to look with favor on the Church, on believers, on the Crimean Tatars, the Volga Germans, the Jews, and on the rights of other minorities.

PO   It was just as the Chinese foresaw: when Khrushchev threw out the dirty bath water, he all but threw out the baby with it; by that I mean the credibility of Soviet power. Didn't Khrushchev and his cohorts try at least to reconcile this contradiction?

RM   Khrushchev and his cohorts were sure that they could hold the anti-Stalin reaction within limits that suited them. But when they saw that the adverse criticism was going too far, that it was probing too deeply into the very structure of the ruling power, they tried to soft-pedal it. But let me point out one significant fact: that as a rule, not even the most vituperative denunciations of Stalinism cast any doubts on socialism or on the guiding role of the party; they didn't threaten Soviet power as such; but understandably, the growing animosity toward Stalinism did threaten the power of those men who shared in the responsibility for his crimes. The Chinese were all wrong when they faulted the policies adopted by the Twentieth and Twenty-Second congresses. The truth is that they feared the possible effect of those two events on the Chinese people.

PO   You began working on your book about Stalinism at that time. As we have seen, you had no trouble with it at first, but your difficulties mounted as time passed until the party expelled you. It seems to me, therefore, that the story of the book up to its publication in the West illustrates the change in attitude of the authorities in terms of the debate on Stalinism. I mean that those in power, by designating themselves the only authentic interpreters of the Sta-

64

linist phenomenon, in reality were trying to prevent the nation and the most free-thinking elements from confronting a problem of far greater importance—that is, the search for a theory of a new and more human socialism and its implementation . . .

RM I agree with you, but again only in part. In those years, the government not only refused to encourage middle-range researchers to work independently in the field of general theory but curbed their freedom by every possible means, and sometimes persecuted them. My position was privileged because I wasn't a historian by profession but an instructor performing the duties assigned me by the plan at my place of work and writing my book only in my spare time. That's why for a long time no one came to ask me what I was doing, and none of my superiors could interfere. But eventually the local and city committees caught up with me because I was enrolled in the party.

In pre-Stalin times, Lenin wasn't the only part theoretician; many other prominent Bolsheviks also studied theoretical problems: Trotsky, Bukharin, Kamenev, Lunacharsky, and so on. A good many other party functionaries worked with considerable latitude as theoretical researchers in the social sciences. But by the beginning of the '30s, a situation had been created whereby the sole exponent of fundamental Marxist theory was Stalin himself. It was acknowledged that only Stalin had the right to propose new theoretical principles; no one else could do anything more than comment on Marxist-Leninist-Stalinist thought and propagate it. The result, of course, was a period of stagnation in theoretical research and a crisis in all the social sciences.

But even after Stalin's death under the "collective leadership" the plight of the social sciences didn't improve very much because the new government perpetuated Stalin's principle of hierarchy, which holds that only the party leadership can interpret the history of the Soviet Communist Party, Marxist theory, and scientific socialism.

PO What you're saying is: that it's not ideology but rather the infallibility of the ruling powers, who reinterpret it from time to time, that constitutes the real instrument of social control over the Soviet people, right?

RM   Ideology is enormously important in the USSR, but much depends on how an ideological concept is interpreted at any given moment. That's because only those who command real power over the state and the ideological apparatus may carry out the function of authentic interpreting.

But you must understand that not all their conclusions contradict what Marx, Engels, and Lenin said. The founders of Marxism-Leninism were scientists as well as politicians. They modified their ideas as time passed, conditions changed, and new logic came to light with the development of scientific thought. That's why you'll find that Marx, Engels, and Lenin would interpret a single problem in three different ways. But there are many people who, when they construe ideology in their own versions, formulate principles that conflict sharply both in spirit and letter with what those men believed. This doesn't mean that they're abandoning dogma or the development of Marxism-Leninism, but the contrary: often they make the dogmatic nature of various ideological propositions more rigid.

PO   Marx would have said that this is how ideology is reduced to false consciousness . . .

RM   Yes. Marx surely wouldn't have been happy to observe the fate that has befallen many aspects of his teaching. At the end of his life, when he saw how some of his principles were being arbitrarily interpreted and reinterpreted, he said with a sigh, "If that's Marxism, I'm no Marxist." If he were still with us, he would be less disturbed by the fact that many of his predictions never came to pass and many of his assertions have proved to be erroneous than to see how his thought has been reduced to dogma and how people interpret him so arbitrarily and in such bad faith.

6

Division among
the Dissidents

PO Let's go back to the '70s. Sinyavsky and Daniel have been tried, Tvardovsky has left *Novy Mir*, all Khrushchev's concessions have been abrogated, the innovations he set in motion arrested. Brezhnev has been in power for six years, he now feels fully secure in his preeminence, and he devises a strategy of his own to combat dissent. What were the first visible symptoms of this new strategy?

RM I don't know that Brezhnev and his collaborators worked out a new strategy of their own. I can only surmise by what happened and what I observed from below as a participant in the movement. Judging from what I saw, probably the worst years were 1968–70, that is right after the Warsaw Pact troops invaded Czechoslovakia. That was the moment of the pro- and neo-Stalinist offensive, when the government cracked down on the dissidents . . . in 1967 their number was relatively high . . . and tormented them with harrowing reprisals of every sort.

Brezhnev established his undisputed supremacy around the summer of 1970 when he began implementing his policy of détente,

67

first with the nations of Western Europe, shortly after with the United States; this policy achieved its logical fruition with the Helsinki agreements. I'd say that the years between 1971 and 1976 were relatively easy on the dissidents. Certainly the pressures continued, and many persons were put on trial, but to a noticeably lesser extent. In many cases, the authorities didn't arrest dissidents but sent them out of the country instead.

During that time, about 130,000 Jews left the Soviet Union, also tens of thousands of Volga Germans and hundreds of other nationals. Emigration is another method of suppressing dissent. Of course, most dissidents preferred expatriation to arrest, and it benefited the government too, because it put no obstacles in the way of détente. Therefore, if you want to define a Brezhnev strategy, you can say that it prohibited free agitation within the country but countered it more elastically than before by resolving the problem with a minimum of clamor, hence with a minimum of international complications. Thus, the "silent diplomacy" urged by Kissinger and the other Western leaders on the issue of dissent was eminently appropriate.

Now Carter, with his "new approach" to the question of civil rights in countries all over the world, has publicly censured the Soviet government for violating those rights; but let's not forget that the Nixon administration also dealt with the problem and achieved good results with its "silent diplomacy."

But early in 1977, conditions changed again when the regime took a more rigid stand against dissenters . . . I refer to the arrests of Aleksandr Ginzburg, Anatoly Shcharansky, Yuri Orlov, and others. Also, it virtually destroyed the small group of dissidents on the committee monitoring the government's compliance with the terms of the Helsinki agreements, eliminated the fund for political prisoners set up by Solzhenitsyn back in 1974, and suppressed the Soviet branch of Amnesty International. This gave the impression that the government was determined to liquidate the dissident movement, already debilitated by emigration, or at least reduce it to the minimum. Recently, the Writers' Union threw out a dozen members it had hitherto tolerated.

68

PO Does all this mean that the government is less stable than before?
In other words, is it true that the more entrenched the government
is, the more freedom it allows the dissidents, and vice versa, the
less stable it feels, the less it will countenance dissent?

RM I wouldn't say that. The past few decades of Soviet history show no
evidence of any relationship between the stability of government
power and the persecution of dissidents. Stalin began liquidating
millions of potential or imaginary enemies just when his power became practically absolute. Until he arrived at unlimited autocracy,
he was in no position to annihilate almost all the old Leninist
guard. And another thing: we cried out loudest against Stalin's
blunders and crimes when Khrushchev hadn't yet firmly established his authority. Then too, the Soviet press attacked
Khrushchev for his most notorious failures and mistakes . . .
without mentioning his name . . . in 1965–66 before the new
regime had acquired full stability and when a certain struggle was
still going on at the top within the collective leadership.

In our country, it's most often true that the more firmly consolidated the government is, the less it's inclined to tolerate criticism
of its actions . . . although the opposite can also be true, of
course. It was fear of the Prague Spring's destabilizing impact and
a lack of sufficient stability within the Soviet power structure itself
that brought on the invasion of Czechoslovakia.

PO From 1970 on, the dissidents were less harassed, yet they began to
split. Tvardovsky didn't share Solzhenitsyn's reaction to his expulsion from the Writers' Union, Solzhenitsyn took an autonomous
position, and so did Sakharov and you yourself. Why did the dissidents break up just at that moment?

RM That was a logical outcome of the very nature of the movement.
But practically all of us were united in denouncing the past, insist-
ing on the need for changes, and fighting . . . and we're still fighting . . . for a greater measure of human rights in the USSR: the
right to receive and give out information, freedom of speech, recognition of the rights of the Crimean Tatars, freedom of movement, and so on.

69

When Solzhenitsyn wrote his famous 1967 letter to the Fourth
Congress of Soviet Writers, calling for the abolition of censorship,
he won the dissidents' unanimous support. Everywhere they
quoted his words:

> Under the obfuscating label of Glavlit, this censorship—which is not
> provided for in the Constitution and is therefore illegal, and which is
> nowhere publicly labeled as such—imposes a yoke on our literature
> and gives people unversed in literature arbitrary control over writers.
> A survival of the Middle Ages, this censorship has managed, Methu-
> selah-like, to drag out its existence almost to the twenty-first century.
> Of fleeting significance, it attempts to appropriate to itself the role of
> unfleeting time—that of separating good books from bad.

This letter hit the censors as hard as Tvardovsky's poem had;
and Tvardovsky told me himself that he wholly endorsed Solzhenitsyn's demands.

When Sakharov wrote an appeal in 1972 asking the Presidium of
the Supreme Soviet to proclaim a political amnesty, all the dissidents he turned to signed the letter. By then, the dissidents had
arrived as different points of view on various important issues, but
their divergencies didn't stop them from protesting as one against
the violation of human rights.

But to every current of dissent and every faction came the moment not only to protest but also to rethink their "positive" political platforms in greater depth. This is what gave rise to their differences, sometimes to outright rupture. I won't stop to talk about
the actions of some dissidents who, in the course of their struggle,
simply changed their views and convictions. This is especially true
of Sakharov, as he himself wrote in detail and with sincerity in his
autobiography. Again in 1970, together with Sakharov and Turchin, I signed a long letter to Brezhnev, Kosygin, and Podgorny,
urging them to give our country democracy. But I couldn't do
otherwise than disassociate myself from Sakharov when he proclaimed his loss of faith in socialism and spoke out against the
withdrawal of American troops from Vietnam, reproaching the
United States for failing to make a strong enough military effort in
Southeast Asia.

Neither could I fail to disagree with one of my old comrades when, after the [September 1973] *coup* in Chile, he said that Pinochet's dictatorship was a lesser evil than the authoritarian rule of Allende and the Communists. Or again two years later when the tragedy of Chile was obvious to everyone, and that same person declared that "it's better to live under Pinochet than Brezhnev." And how could one fail to repudiate Vladimir Maksimov's argument that Willy Brandt had betrayed the cause of democracy by launching his *Ostpolitik* and therefore should never have been awarded the Nobel Peace Prize but tried instead as a war criminal in some future Nuremberg trial. Again, how could anyone go along with Solzhenitsyn when, in his sadly famous *Letter to the Soviet Leaders*, he proposed founding an authoritarian, theocratic state in the USSR and transferring the whole Russian population to uninhabited territories in northeast Siberia, there to begin a new life without cities, big industries, railroads, automobiles, and democracy? Or when he assailed the censorship of literature but thought it should be applied to political works?

No!

Under such circumstances, rifts among the dissidents were inevitable.

PO   One could judge those rifts from two points of view: as a weakening of the dissident movement under the pressure of the regime and/or as a display of pluralism—that is, as a "spy" for a social articulation far more advanced than it appears to be on the surface.

RM   Division is unavoidably weakening the dissident movement because it's harder to promote common initiatives today, also because the clashes of opinions affect personal relationships negatively. But the same sort of thing has happened throughout history in all currents of opposition. For the government a fractured opposition is a boon.

On the other hand, it reflects the different viewpoints that society nurtures in its very depths. But in Soviet society, these differences aren't as acute as they are among the dissidents, and they involve ordinary citizens only to a very limited extent. Therefore,

71

it's premature to talk about an objective undermining of the prevailing power's despotic character.

PO   When I asked you that question, what I had in mind was this: if the dissidents are split, then we can imagine that the authorities are also. In fact, you yourself have mentioned three groups within the Soviet leadership: the neo-Stalinists, the moderates, and the democrats. Now then . . . given the open rifts among the dissidents and the secret rifts among the leaders, is it reasonable to interpret them as a symptom of a society more polycentric than the government wants us to know about?

RM   Without any doubt, Soviet society is by no means united, and there's more dissatisfaction than the leaders are willing to divulge. But it's not a question of pluralism in the Western sense of the term. Within the regime, the two currents I call neo-Stalinist and democratic lost a good deal of their strength since 1969–70. The Politburo got rid of men like Shelest, Voronov, and Polyansky, considered hard-liners in domestic as well as foreign policy . . . and for good reason. The democrats in the party were already pretty weak, and many of those I believed to be exponents of that current have either quit the Central Committee apparatus of their own volition or have been dismissed from it and transferred to all kinds of scientific institutes.

PO   In any event, the regime always presents a monolithic image of itself to the dissidents. However, could you single out any leaders who are more liberal-minded on the issue of dissent?

RM   Yes indeed, the regime does put up a monolithic front for the dissidents. Some of our bosses don't like us. But they can't agree on how to crush us: some insist on tougher methods, some on softer methods. I can't really name names, but I think that Brezhnev's [neo-Stalinist] advisers like Trapeznikov and Golikov give him less intelligent counsel than others do, like Aleksandrov and Tsukanov. According to rumor, Suslov is more hawk than dove.

PO   When you discuss the dissident movement, you often refer to the Prague Spring and its ultimate fate. What does Dubček's "socialism with a human face" mean to you Soviet dissenters?

72

RM   I cherish the Prague Spring experiment, and so do many of my
      friends because it set its sights on goals that lie close to our hearts.
      It proved that within the Communist Party there are regenerative
      forces that, within a short time, can produce formidable results in
      liberalizing the regime without renouncing the fundamental values
      of socialism. In spite of its short life, that experiment demonstrated
      how important democracy is to socialism and how important social-
      ism is to democracy.

PO   In some people's minds, the Warsaw Pact's invasion of Czechoslo-
      vakia showed that the Soviet government sets precise limits beyond
      which no process of emancipation can go without endangering the
      stability of the system. What are those limits?

RM   I don't think it's possible to give that question any single answer.
      What stability did the Prague Spring endanger? If we refer to
      Novotny's Stalinist despotism,* then certainly the Czech liberals
      overstepped the limits when they tore it down. But the changes
      they introduced couldn't have undermined the stability of social-
      ism itself. Only the dogmatists in the Soviet Embassy in Prague
      could have believed such a thing . . . and with a man at their head
      as totally ignorant of conditions in the country as Ambassador
      Chervonenko was, and as lacking in perspicacity, not to speak of
      some Soviet leaders who were misled by distorted information they
      received from Chervonenko and his deputy, Udaltsov. I'm quite
      sure that if the same changes had been made in Czechoslovakia in
      1972–73, say, instead of 1968, there wouldn't have been any in-
      vasion.
         Many Soviet dissidents saw those events in Czechoslovakia and
      the Soviet invasion as a decisive victory for Stalinism, and they
      feared that it would flash the signal for a new wave of repression in
      the USSR. We had no real movement for solidarity with Czechoslo-
      vakia; only five persons demonstrated in behalf of the Czech re-
      formers. There were no collective letters, no stands taken, no pro-
      tests. This gives ample testimony to the feeble state of the dissident
      movement.

      * Antonin Novotny—Stalinist boss of Czechoslovakia until his removal in January 1968,
      marking the beginning of the Prague Spring.

PO   You think that the experiment in Czechoslovakia was premature . . .

RM   Well, it grew logically out of the country's political evolution, but it should have been handled differently. The Czechs were impatient. The reform process that began to affect world Communism after the Twentieth and Twenty-Second Congresses was too slow for them, and Dubček, not realizing this, committed a number of tactical errors. At first the Czech movement caught on almost spontaneously, with no program worked out beforehand. Probably no one involved in it was prepared for the role he would play in the turbulent succession of events that followed. You can't blame Dubček or his close collaborators. It was simply a matter of bad luck. If they had moved faster and held their Fourteenth party congress* in June, or even May, and rid their Central Committee of the dogmatists and Stalinists . . . those who later "invited" the Soviet troops into Czechoslovakia . . . the invasion would have been impossible for a number of political . . . and nonpolitical . . . reasons. Or vice versa, Dubček should have moved more slowly and with greater prudence, and taken into account what the reactions of the countries bordering on Czechoslovakia would be, to give them no pretext whatever for the invasion.

PO   I've heard it said that dissent in the Eastern European countries differs from the Soviet brand for historical and political reasons. With the October Revolution in Russia, nationalism and Communism went hand-in-hand, they coincided. But in Eastern Europe, Communism was imported from abroad . . . and by the Red Army . . . therefore, the local populations see it as the invader's ideology. In those countries, Communism and nationalism do not coincide, they diverge. In this context, Soviet dissent is essentially ideological whereas in the satellite countries it's primarily nationalistic. What do you say to this interpretation?

---

* Fourteenth Congress of the Communist Party of Czechoslovakia—held secretly in Prague after, and in protest against, the Soviet invasion of August 1968. Its resolutions, strongly opposed to the old Stalinist methods and favoring democratization, were later repudiated by the Husak leadership.

RM I don't agree. It oversimplifies and confuses many highly complex
problems, for which there isn't any one solution. It's true that the
Czechoslovak people are painfully unhappy about their depen-
dence on the USSR, and that the invasion they never expected left
a festering wound in their national pride. So their dissident movement is unmistakably national in character. But look here . . . did
the Red Army really import Communism into the country, and does
the population see it as the ideology of a conqueror? Before World
War II, Communism was already a powerful force in Czechoslovakia, and the party's influence was dominant during the war years.
The majority of the population approved Klement Gottwald's* first
government.

As for Yugoslavia, can anyone say that Communist ideology and
the Communist government were imposed by "foreign conquest"?
With Tito at its head, the Yugoslav Communist Party controlled
practically the whole country by the end of the war. In Bulgaria,
too, the Communist movement was going strong even before the
war.

In Poland, the situation was more complex. There the Communist Party was actually liquidated when its leaders, who were living
in Moscow, were shot, and the Comintern dissolved the Polish
party. Things were also different in Hungary and Romania, where
the Communist parties hardly counted at the end of hostilities. The
Soviet Union's interference in their domestic affairs was indeed
onerous, but it was justified if only because these two countries
fought on Hitler's side; they were aggressors and the Red Army defeated them on the battlefield. The same goes for East Germany,
where Soviet occupation was sanctioned by the four-power agreement of the Allies at the end of World War II.

You can't say that Communism and nationalism coincided in the
USSR immediately after the October revolution: that identification
didn't begin until later, and it was never complete. In the Eastern
European dissident movements, the national factor certainly fig-

* Head of the Communist Party of Czechoslovakia when it took power in 1948; became
president of the country at that time.

ures prominently but probably no more so than in the Ukraine or the Baltic republics. On the whole, their dissidents' most pressing demands are the same as ours: more democracy, pluralism, and the right to receive and give out information. But there are no organizational links between the Soviet and Eastern European dissidents, only moral solidarity.

PO Do you think that at some future time the various dissident movements in the USSR and the satellite countries in Europe will be able to establish ties and some effective form of collaboration? In times to come could the common basis . . . the demand for more democracy . . . become a unifying factor, on organizational and other levels, that would affect the stability of the Soviet system?

RM It's extremely difficult to foresee the future of dissent in the USSR and other Communist countries. Today the movement is fragmented; it's in a stage of temporary crisis. Cooperation, a meeting of opinions, and the links binding together the different factions presuppose a degree of liberalization granted by the respective governments, and no such liberalization yet exists. The dissident movement must be legalized in the USSR and elsewhere; it's virtually impossible to maintain clandestine ties.*

* Certain limited ties have begun to be formed among dissidents in Soviet-bloc countries. In January 1979 a representative of a Polish dissident group, the Social Self-Defense Committee (better known by its earlier name, Workers Defense Committee—Polish initials, KOR), was able to visit Moscow. There he held discussions with Sakharov and other Soviet civil-rights activists. In these discussions, according to the New York-based *Chronicle of Human Rights in the USSR*, the KOR representative and the Soviet dissidents exchanged information and "established principles of cooperation."

In July 1979 a joint statement was issued by the Helsinki Watch Group in Moscow and the Polish KOR calling for the release of ten leaders of the Czechoslovak dissident group Charter 77 who had been arrested in May 1979. A major trial of six of these Charter 77 leaders, apparently aimed at discouraging dissent throughout Eastern Europe, was held in Prague in October 1979. The three most prominent defendants—Petr Uhl, former economist; Vaclav Havel, the playwright; and Vaclav Benda, a human-rights activist—were given prison sentences of five, four and a half, and four years, respectively.

(In the fall of 1978, representatives of Charter 77 and KOR had met three times near the Polish-Czechoslovak border. Among other things, they had issued a joint call for cooperation among oppositionist groups in the various Eastern European countries and Soviet republics.)

7

Socialism Rather
Than Marxism

PO Before discussing the whole ideological spectrum in the dissident
movement, we can say for certain that in theoretical respects it has
two faces. One, with Solzhenitsyn and his followers as exponents,
totally rejects the very nature of Soviet socialism. The other, which
you and those who share your opinion stand for, deplores the
deficiencies in the system but accepts its socialist premises. Do you
agree?

RM The two faces you speak of do indeed exist, but so do many others.
One of the most important involves Sakharov and his disciples.
Neither Sakharov nor his followers make an appeal for any specific political platform, but stress the nonpartisan, apolitical nature of their movement. Rather than propose any doctrine, they
call for strict observance [by the authorities, in practice] of the
laws on paper in the USSR, and observance of the UN conventions
on human rights, to which our government has subscribed. This
movement is a very important one because it gives people without
any ideological orientation a chance to take an active part on the
social level. There are also the lesser currents we've already talked
about.

PO On the subject of Sakharov, let me tell you about an episode that happened to me. Once two Italian Communists came to see me with a Russian friend of theirs. The Italians deprecated Sakharov for having no "world view," no ideology, but the Russian didn't agree with them. He said, "We don't need any more 'world views'; we wouldn't know what to do with them. What we need are real freedoms now, not in a future that will never come." Is this sort of thinking common, and does it figure particularly in dissident circles?

RM Some people entertain ideas of that sort, but I couldn't say how common they are. Sakharov once tried to define his dissent in ideological terms and delved into all kinds of socio-political theories. But then he abandoned this tack in the belief that it was more difficult than mastering contemporary physics and its highly complicated theories. It would be unfair to disparage him for that. After all, no one expects a scientist or a physicist to invent a new doctrine in the realm of social relations any more than a sociologist or "political scientist," as you would say, would be capable of giving the world a new theory in physics.

    The fight Sakharov and his disciples are putting up for human rights and freedoms is a noble one as far as its inspiration goes, but they're doomed to fail if they don't bring forth a doctrine to sustain their ideas. We can't achieve rights and freedoms without transforming our one-party system, with the party itself devising the mechanisms to control and regulate criticisms of its own actions. But you can't change the regime without some concrete program or doctrine. I dare say that in our circumstances, democratic socialism . . . that is, a socialism that embraces pluralism . . . is the only viable doctrine. Only a socialism that tolerates legal opposition to the government and the ruling party can avoid slipping into totalitarianism and abuse of power.

PO I agree with you about the need for a "world view," but allow me to go on acting the devil's advocate. It seems to me that my Russian friend's position doesn't imply a radical negation of any doctrine. In my view, he rejected attempts to fit the reality of historical phe-

78

nomena into world views and philosophies that always fail for the simple reason that they do not constitute "knowledge that is applicable in practice." I think he was advocating a switch from abstract philosophical theory to a pragmatic theory of knowledge and ultimately to politics as "the art of the possible." I'd like to know what you have to say on this point.

RM Here we enter into a purely terminological controversy which isn't easy to carry forward because some words have different connotations. It's useless to take every philosophy as utopian or all politics as realistic. With all its shortcomings, Marxist philosophy has been applied to reality not in a direct and immediate way but rather through political and economic doctrines. These doctrines have changed from epoch to epoch within the framework of a single general Marxist theory. For instance, in 1921 the doctrine of "war communism" gave way to the NEP.* In 1965, in connection with the economic reform, an attempt was made to work out a new doctrine more relevant to the technical and industrial level the country had reached. Let me also say that empirical theory of knowledge is one of the possible forms of philosophical doctrine.

The new political doctrine we need must take into proper account the potentialities within Soviet society, the level of social consciousness we have attained, and our historical experience. In this context, your friend's notion that we don't need doctrines but freedoms seems to indicate a mental attitude more utopian then political, particularly where society's possibilities for development are concerned.

PO So that philosophy for the most part answers the question "why," whereas political science tells us "how." It strikes me that Soviet Marxism has always striven to give an answer to the "why" of Marxism without giving adequate answers to many "hows."

RM I don't agree entirely. The Russian Bolsheviks tried to clarify both the "whys" and the "hows." But only partial answers have been

---

* NEP—the New Economic Policy, introduced in 1921 to replace the "war communism" policy of near total government control of the economy (1918–20). NEP revived elements of a capitalist market economy, especially in agriculture.

SOCIALISM RATHER THAN MARXISM

found. For example, the Soviet Marxists have explained only in part the "why" of both socialism and contemporary capitalism. And there are many world problems today for which Soviet Marxism has never produced satisfactory explanations. This by no means signifies that such questions can't be resolved within the framework of scientific socialism . . . or, as some believe, that they can be resolved by imposing antiquated dogmas. To arrive at the necessary answers, we must still put in a good deal of thought and a good deal of hard work.

I can't go along with you when you say that Soviet Marxism hasn't answered the question "how." Certainly in the USSR we haven't made exhaustive studies and we've committed a lot of mistakes. Our society is developing chaotically in many respects, but it is developing; it isn't standing still. You know that when Lenin led the Bolsheviks in an unprecedented socialist revolution, he openly admitted that they had not yet found an answer to the question "how," and he said that only the experience gained in struggle would produce it. He also said that the Russian revolution was a chain of multiform experiments in one of history's most remarkable ventures, and that the Bolsheviks would probably modify their orientations again and again to tell us "how" with more accuracy. Lenin, for example, from 1917 to 1921, searched with patient persistence for a way to reconcile the interests of the workers and the peasants and avoid a cleavage between the two classes, both opposed to the autocracy and landed aristocracy, yet both pursuing distinctly different goals. He found the solution in the NEP, which answered the question "how" for a long period of time.

Some people believe that no one should experiment with mankind. But revolution is always an experiment, and the whole history of the human race is an endless succession of trial and error. The evolution of man isn't an automatic process; it relies on human will and on the decisions men themselves make. And revolutions spring from the aspiration to improve imperfect and unjust social orders, even if justice and perfection don't always triumph in the end. The road to these ideals is still long and difficult, and new questions will crop up to which we must give new answers.

PO   Now we've come to the heart of the problem. Liberals object to
      Marxism as a "philosophy concerned with ends" rather than a
      "culture built around means," unlike liberalism, which is both.
      Put differently, Marxism, they say, has failed to achieve its ends
      because the means it has used to realize them conflict with those
      ends. I see the Soviet Union as the most pertinent observation post
      for making a reply to this objection.

RM   It's not at all true that Marxism hasn't achieved its ends. Even
      today Marxism has a whole string of successes to its credit. Is there
      any movement in the nineteenth or twentieth centuries that has ar-
      rived at its goals exactly as its founders envisaged them? In any
      case, Marxism continues to thrive and expand while many other
      doctrines have long since vanished from the political scene.
          As for the correlation of means and ends, this is a very complex
      philosophical and practical question, the problem at the core of
      every political doctrine. Marxism hasn't come up with a fully satis-
      factory solution, but we mustn't confuse classical Marxism's theo-
      retical solutions . . . which encompass any number of just and
      honest concepts . . . with Stalinism, which perverted not only its
      means but even its very aims.
          Generally, ends and means don't always correspond. To write a
      good book you must have talent, but you also have to put hard
      work into it. So far, ends and means coincide. But to alleviate the
      suffering of someone who is critically ill, we often tell him untruths
      about his condition; we deliberately deceive him. Here you have a
      contradiction between ends and means, yet no one will castigate his
      doctor or his relatives for their motives.
          To combat crime and violence, every government in the world
      resorts to violence, a method the United Nations itself endorses.
      Marxist doctrine doesn't rule out revolutionary violence or a revo-
      lutionary war in the struggle for socialism, but it rejects the princi-
      ple that *any means whatever* are permissible toward that end, just
      as international conventions ban certain methods of waging war, of
      treating prisoners of war, and so on. Similarly, there must be
      limits to revolutionary violence. Nowadays people who hijack

81

planes and hold innocent hostages call themselves revolutionists, but every really revolutionary party deplores such crimes.

PO   Going back to the dissident movement . . . Solzhenitsyn says that personal, social, and national repentance always purifies the atmosphere. He thinks that if we frankly recognize the horrors of our past and repudiate them with all our strength, not with empty words, our country will gain a greater measure of trust in the world. In practical terms, what does he have in mind?

RM   Every crime must be censured, whether committed in the past by governments or populations with which we have no connection or committed in our time in any part of the world. If we state the problem in these general terms, then obviously we must agree with Solzhenitsyn. We still decry the bloodthirsty Roman emperors, the Greek tyrants, and the criminals who executed Archimedes, Giordano Gruno, Servetus, and Lavoisier as well as those who murdered Nikolai Vavilov, García Lorca, and Osip Mandelstam. But when Solzhenitsyn declares that all revolutions in the past and present should be denounced indiscriminately, I can't go along with him.

Of course, repentance, both individual and national, purifies the atmosphere, but only those guilty of a crime can and must pay the price. Solzhenitsyn, however, wants all individuals and nations to repent the crimes of their remote ancestors; and when he cites the reciprocal guilt of two peoples toward each other, he goes to an absurd extreme. "The Tatar yoke on Russia," he wrote in *From Under the Rubble*, "will attenuate *forever* our guilt toward the descendants of the Horde." But the Crimean Tatars are descendants of the Horde, and if we recall how medieval khans in the Crimea repeatedly ravaged Russian territory, at the time free of the Tatar yoke, then . . . if we listen to Solzhenitsyn . . . can we reasonably denounce Stalin for deporting the Tatars from the Crimea? In some cases, sons should certainly redeem the sins of their fathers, and in others, a population should make reparation for the evils inflicted by their forebears on other populations in the more or less

82

recent past; but all these questions of morality are far more complex than Solzhenitsyn would have it seem. The rite of repentance,
which he stresses more than the other Christian rituals, won't
always repair the damage. One could cite a thousand examples of
men and women who have repented and then gone back to repeat-
ing their sins over and over again.

PO If you'll allow me, for the sake of convenience I'd like to sum up
Solzhenitsyn's moral and political philosophy, which proceeds
from an ethical concept of socialism . . . or rather, from a solidarism deriving from Christian universalism and eternalism. In his
view, future Soviet society cannot be based on a principle of hatred, such as the class-struggle concept, but must arise from another criterion: Is everything we do, have done, and will do moral?
Is our whole life moral? I'd like you to tell me how Solzhenitsyn arrived at this conception.

RM Solzhenitsyn's philosophy is so contradictory that it's hard to sum-
marize it. He formulates different viewpoints at different times.
Early in the '60s when *Novy Mir* proposed him for the Lenin Prize,
he repeatedly exalted Lenin in his conversations with prominent
Soviet writers and he said nothing against accepting a prize that
bore Lenin's name. Apart from a few intimate friends, no one
knew about his deep religious feelings; Tvardovsky, for one, never
suspected anything of the sort. And in discussions of *Cancer
Ward*, he never demurred when anyone labeled him a champion of
ethical socialism. As people who have read *Cancer Ward* will recall, Shulubin, one of the characters in the novel, talks about the
need for ethical socialism. But today Solzhenitsyn stoutly opposes
both ethical socialism and socialism in general. He has said again
and again that the confusion between his own ideas and those of
his characters is a pure misunderstanding.

As for his Christianity, it's too belligerent and implacable to
relate to Christian universalism and solidarism. In his *forma
mentis* Solzhenitsyn is a "Bolshevik in reverse," indeed one of the
most extreme. Hs portrait of Lenin in *Lenin in Zurich* doesn't

83

resemble the man very much, although there are some elements of similarity; it's more like Solzhenitsyn himself, as many critics who reviewed the book pointed out.

PO Still, Solzhenitsyn's ideas are nothing new in the history of Russian culture, are they?

RM With all the respect I have for that great writer's creative talent, I find it hard to believe in the sincerity of his moral preachments. Anyway, if we accept your definition of Solzhenitsyn's ideas and philosophy as a hypothesis, yes, I will say that it conforms to Russian cultural tradition.

By the middle of the nineteenth century, two trends were emerging in Russian intellectual circles. One insisted on a revolutionary transformation of Russia and the violent overthrow of the autocracy. The other called for a moral regeneration based on nationalist and Pan-Slavic values and Orthodox Christianity. In my opinion, it was Russia that gave the world the greatest religious philosophers of the twentieth century, such as Sergei Bulgakov, Vladimir Solovyov, and Nikolai Berdyaev. In 1909 it was from such religious and philosophical circles that the anthology *Vekhi* (Milestones) came, which stirred up a heated controversy among the intelligentsia.* The same authors contributed to another anthology, *From the Depths*, published in 1918 and reissued in 1967 by the YMCA Press in Paris. Carrying on this tradition, in 1975 Solzhenitsyn and his group published abroad a collection entitled *From Under the Rubble*, which has not made the same kind of stir either in the USSR or outside.

Now then . . . and here I omit any judgment on values . . . it's a fact that the Russian people have moved forward, not by way of religious uplift, but through revolution; and despite all the disap-

---

* *Vekhi*—Most of the contributors, among them Bulgakov and Berdyaev, had been prominent liberals calling for a constitutional regime during the 1905–07 revolution in Russia; earlier some had been Marxists. In light of the failure of the revolution, in *Vekhi* they denounced the whole radical and revolutionary tradition in Russia and called on the intelligentsia to renounce materialism, turn to religion, support the tsarist government, and accept Russian nationalism. This provoked heated denunciations of them as renegades.

pointments they've encountered on the way, they'll leave our descendants not a religious heritage but socialism and democracy, even if the alternative possibility of continued authoritarian socialism cannot be excluded.

PO   But don't you think that Solzhenitsyn's arguments give voice to a real demand of the Russian people, to their profound sense of religion, the need, felt by so many, for an authentic moral and political participation? I don't see that either Marxism theoretically or Soviet socialism historically have given a satisfactory response on this score.

RM   I must acknowledge that ethics has always been the weakest aspect of Marxism. Marx assimilated and elaborated on English political economy, French utopian socialism, and classical German philosophy, but he underestimated the ethical function of religion. Marxism and scientific socialism, however, are not synonymous: the concept of scientific socialism is much broader than the Marxist concept. Socialism certainly doesn't mean amorality; a socialist society can gradually evolve its own ethical code, based not on divine revelations but on reason, conscience, human justice, and universal precepts of good and evil.

In the USSR, the church and religion haven't completely lost their venerable prestige, and I think they should be given due latitude to reveal fully all their potential values.

PO   Let's go back to Solzhenitsyn. Why did the government drive him out of the Soviet Union? Why did it want to be rid of him?

RM   I can't easily speak for the government, although I try to understand what it has in mind. I think the authorities decided to expel Solzhenitsyn only when they discovered the content of *The Gulag Archipelago*. Before that he vowed that under no circumstances would he emigrate; in fact he condemned those Russian dissidents who did; consequently the world understood his emigration to be forced exile. For reasons we can well imagine, the government felt that a trial against him wouldn't be feasible.

Early in the '20s, a clause was added to the RSFSR penal code

85

that provided for the forced expatriation of counter-revolutionaries and persons agitating against the Soviet power. Expulsion was then equated with death by a firing squad—the most extreme forms of punishment. This clause was retained in the penal code until 1961, when a new code was adopted, but in practice it was applied only in 1922–23. Well, it might have been applied from time to time during the '20s, but certainly in the '30s and later, never. The last person to be expelled from the USSR was Trotsky, in 1929.

In his novel *The First Circle*, Solzhenitsyn describes a mock trial held by a group of convicts as a joke. Their victim is a Russian prince, Igor Svyatoslavich, the hero of a famous Russian epic, who was captured by a Tatar khan. The "tribunal," selected by the convicts, pokes fun at the absurd Stalinist judicial procedure, and condemns Igor Svyatoslavich, under Article 20a of the penal code, "to expulsion from the borders of the USSR as an enemy of the workers." When the sentence is pronounced, the prisoners greet it with an explosion of laughter.

Certainly Solzhenitsyn never dreamed that the same verdict would be pronounced against him. I believe that in his case, the Presidium of the Supreme Soviet passed a special resolution which, in the USSR, is tantamount to law.

PO Why hasn't the Presidium given Sakharov the same treatment?

RM I don't know whether or not the ruling powers intend to send him into exile. Sakharov, you know, was denied permission to go to Norway to receive the Nobel Peace Prize in 1975 because he'd had access to important state secrets in the past. In our military industry, men who carry out sensitive functions like those given to Sakharov must sign a commitment that they will not go abroad or enter into contact with foreigners for a period of fifteen years without authorization by their superiors. I believe that many military secrets Sakharov knew about are still important today.

PO You prefer to call yourself a socialist rather than a Marxist because you say that Marxism has often been imprecise and made mistakes, which a nondogmatic Marxist must rectify in order to

86

deal with the problems faced by the society in which he lives. In what sense does the term "Marxist" fail to define contemporary socialist thought adequately?

RM   All through the history of science we come across cases in which some brilliant scientist hits on an important discovery or works out a new theory, thereby laying the foundation for a new discipline. Copernicus, for one, provided the basis for scientific astronomy, and in the decades that followed, all those who shared his theory called themselves Copernicans. Darwin gave us scientific biology, and for years thereafter all biologists who followed him called themselves Darwinians. Newton originated the science of mechanics and likewise, for a long time, his disciples referred to themselves as Newtonians. Marx introduced a radical new direction in the social sciences when he made a series of momentous discoveries concerning political economy and the material basis of the historical process. Naturally, all those who accepted the precepts of Marx and his friend Engels began to call themselves Marxists. Naming whole disciplines and scientific trends after their respective founders is one way of recognizing their genius. But the name doesn't necessarily last indefinitely. Today scientists who study the movements of celestial bodies call themselves simply astronomers, those who study the actions of terrestrial bodies are physicists, and those who study the animal and vegetable world are biologists.

Marx and Engels opened up significant new avenues in the social sciences, so I have no objection to being called a Marxist. But in the last hundred years [i.e., since their time], countless new problems have arisen in the social sciences, which cannot go unheeded . . . In the middle of the nineteenth century, no one could have imagined them, and neither Marx nor Engels nor Lenin ever expressed any opinion on them. Some have been resolved in a very approximate way, sometimes erroneously, but that's not to be wondered at; it happens in the evolution of every science.

To indicate the development of the social sciences more clearly, I prefer the term *scientific socialism* to *Marxism-Leninism*, which by no means diminishes the role of Marx and Engels as its founders,

87

nor does it belittle Lenin's contribution to the development of their theories.

PO   There's one odd contradiction in the history of Marxism: the principle that, more than any other, attributes to the "nameless forces" of history, that is the masses, an importance decisive to social progress. But Marxism is the only modern mass movement to bear the name of its founder, and to have a history strictly identified with a single personality and his cult. How do you explain this?

RM   All through the history of mankind, ideas have been named after their originators, and some still are today. Confucianism continues to be a very real force in the political and moral life of that immense country, China, even though Confucius lived more than two thousand years ago. The same is true of Buddhism, Christianity, and so on. They began not only as religious but ethico-political movements as well. Therefore, Marxism isn't the only political movement that carries the name of its founder. Leaving aside such variants of Marxism as Leninism, Maoism, and Trotskyism, what about Gandhiism?

Marxism, as we know, certainly didn't start out as *ideology*. Neither Marx nor Engels liked that approach. They worked out a scientific conception that searched for answers to the problems of their times. But the development of their theory coincided with the birth and rise of a new class, the proletariat, with turbulent, revolutionizing changes in the lives of enormous masses of people, and with the emergence of political parties. All this created the conditions for the dogmatization of Marxism, for its transformation into a dogmatic political and philosophical doctrine, and for the rise of a cult of Marx even while he was still alive, despite his firm opposition. The cult of Marx is often exploited to smuggle in, under the Marxist label, concepts and principles that have nothing to do with his true teachings.

I repeat, Marxism didn't begin as ideology. In one of their first great works, *The German Ideology*, Marx and Engels refer to ideology disparagingly as "false consciousness." And in many of his later works, Marx refers to it as a distorted reflection of reality. In *Capital* he constantly gives the term a negative connotation. You will find the same thing in Engels' *Anti-Dühring*.

Anyway, like all other socio-political concepts, you can use the word "ideology" in various ways. In the socialist countries today, the term "ideology" . . . or "Marxist-Leninist ideology" . . . has taken on a significance altogether different from its original meaning: false consciousness. It has become a means of systematizing the teachings of Marx and Engels into rigid dogma. Therefore, I prefer the phrase "scientific socialism" to "Marxist-Leninist ideology."

PO Most of the doctrines you spoke of that bear the names of their originators lean heavily toward dogmatism. Let me ask you this: are Leninism, Stalinism, and now Brezhnevism dogmatic versions of Marxism? And doesn't substituting the term "socialist" for "Marxist" imply a transition from an old political concept to a new one?

RM That's a very involved question, but let me answer it this way: When the teachings of a great scientist or preacher acquire immense authority and attract millions of people, many later disciples, even the best of them, will try to introduce modifications to conform with the new times and new conditions, but without abandoning the Master's fundamental principles or dropping the old name of the movement. Yet those who depart totally from the founder's ideas usually continue to identify themselves as his disciples.

Stalinism had practically nothing in common with Marxism except terminology; yet Stalin continued to call himself a Marxist. We find the same thing with religious doctrines. Today we have countless denominations: Catholic, Orthodox, Protestant, Baptist, Evangelist, and so on, all calling themselves Christian. I don't know that there's such a thing as Khrushchevism or Brezhnevism. Neither Khrushchev nor Brezhnev brought any concept of their own to Marxist doctrine, nor did they profess to.

As everyone knows, Mao Zedong, on the other hand, wanted to

89

be taken as a great theorist in the sphere of Marxist thought and, in fact, beginning in the early '30s, he shaped his own concept of the Chinese revolution and a Chinese version of Marxism. Without going into how much error there is in his theories, I only wish to stress that he adapted Marxism to the Chinese scene in a completely original way, which contributed to the initial great success of the Chinese revolution.

In Europe I think one can speak of Titoism; and recently a new variant of Marxism has been developing at a rapid pace. This is Eurocommunism, so-called, and without doubt a great future lies ahead for it in Western Europe.

The identification of a theory with one person inevitably contributes to its dogmatization. I consider it a good sign that so far Eurocommunism has avoided this kind of personal identification.

When I say that it's high time for the Communist parties to pass on from "Marxism-Leninism" to the broader vision of "scientific socialism" I mean that this would reduce the danger of dogmatic Communist ideology and would increase the possibility for progress and improvement in these parties' theoretical work.

PO   Yes, but there's another side to the problem. All the "isms" in the Marxist movement have coincided historically with as many attempts to give concrete application to the Marxist utopia. From this we must deduce that these "isms" are the equivalent in Marxism to secularization [in Church history], the "institutional road" by which Marxism is realized; in essence, they are the specific working instruments of Marxist theory.

RM   I don't think that's so. Marx always saw his theory as a philosophy of action. Therefore from the very outset Marxism searched not only for the solution to this or that scientific problem but also for a way to radically transform the contemporary world, the entire political and economic reality. In his *Theses on Feuerbach* Marx, still a young man, wrote, "The philosophers have only *interpreted* the world in various ways; the point is to *change* it." This task he expounds in detail in the *Communist Manifesto*. Toward that transformation, he and Engels elaborated not only theories but also a

90

plan for practical action, from creating the Communist League in
the initial stage to establishing the International, or what we call
the First International, which brought various workers' parties
together in a single organization.

   The emergence of the various "isms" related to the movement's
need to grapple with the new tasks it faced in the different countries to keep pace with the rapid development of the capitalist and,
now today, the socialist systems. Often the "isms" represent such
variation on Marx's original theory that they affect its very content. In Russia, for example, the guiding force of the revolution
from 1905 on was the working class because the Bolsheviks had no
nuclei in the rural districts until 1917. In China it was just the reverse. For twenty years the party rested on the peasant movement;
in fact it was actually in the rural areas that the basic cadres of the
party were formed from 1929 to 1949. In Russia the city liberated
the countryside, while in China the countryside liberated the city.
You can go on and on citing similar examples.

PO   We'll say, then, that the many "isms" originated in the universal-
ity of Marx's thought. And this raises two very pertinent questions.
Did Stalinism have its origin in both Marxism and Leninism? And
are the Soviet leaders justified when they claim to be Marx's most
direct heirs?

RM   Assuredly there were some elements of both Marxism and Leninism
in Stalinism. And obviously, if Stalin had not continued to use
Marxist terminology, he could not have forged ahead or main-
tained his power within the party. But here we should distinguish
between words and deeds. It was typical of Stalin to say one thing
and do just the opposite. We need only to read his works to see
that he had a propensity for schematism and scholasticism, and
that he was a dogmatic Marxist. But if we examine his political
record, we find a shrewd and treacherous person who was not at
all dogmatic. He fed on Marx's ideas like a parasite, but he never
put those ideas into practice.

   I haven't read anywhere that our Soviet leaders claim to be the
most direct heirs of Marx any more than the leaders of other Com-

munist parties. Anyway, scrupulously abiding by a Master's dogma in every detail doesn't necessarily mean that you're his best disciple or most direct heir. In Russia it was the Mensheviks who honored Marx's formulas most faithfully, not the Bolsheviks. Only history and experience can determine who has really best continued Marx's ideas and cause.

PO We can absolve Marx on grounds of insufficient proof, but it's harder to absolve Lenin. Both Marxists and non-Marxists say that it was Lenin who introduced many elements into the Soviet political system that Stalin took over and enlarged on: the single party, censorship, intolerance of political opponents, centralism, and party discipline. Can you trace the line of demarcation between Leninism and Stalinism?

RM The political and economic system in the USSR at the beginning of 1918 was much different from what it became at the end of that year, what was later called "war communism." But then at the close of 1921 came NEP, a political and economic system entirely different from "war communism"*—and that happened while Lenin was still alive. There's no doubt that many elements Stalin enlarged on originated under Lenin, or else were introduced with his participation. Those most important were the one-party dictatorship, limitations on discussion within the party, censorship, and greater use of violence against political opponents. But these features are not inherent in the doctrine of Leninism.

Early on, Lenin envisioned Soviet power functioning as a pluralistic system, allowing for free competition within the soviets among all parties representing the workers—the Left Socialist Revolutionaries, Mensheviks, Anarchists, and others. Furthermore, the ban on parties outside the system of soviets was meant at first as a temporary measure. Lenin, you see, was convinced that the Bolsheviks would come out ahead of all the other parties in any free competition, and that the Bolshevik Party . . . considering its po-

*On NEP and "war communism" see note on p. 79.

92

litical and economic successes . . . would easily win the support of the majority. Therefore it could govern with a minimum of violence even in the first phase of the transition period.

But all that was lost because of the sharp conflicts that developed, particularly the civil war. These conflicts broke out not only because the counterrevolutionaries tried to overthrow the Soviet power but also because of the mistakes the Bolsheviks made. At any rate, while the civil war was going on, such measures as increased centralism, tighter discipline, a crackdown on the other parties, militarization of the Bolshevik Party, the introduction of censorship, and the Red Terror—at a certain point, all these factors became a matter of life and death. The question "Who will prevail?" (*kto kogo?*—literally, "Who [will beat] whom?") was posed during the civil war in its most primitive form. Had the Bolsheviks been defeated, all of them would have been physically liquidated.

PO Briefly then, the premises of Stalinism already existed under Lenin, although out of necessity.

RM Stalin took actions that Lenin meant to be only temporary, magnified them and transformed them into permanent procedures. Lenin showed no leniency toward enemies *outside* the party, but Stalin applied this attitude to his opponents *within* the party. Lenin wielded enormous authority, but he was never an autocratic dictator.

I could talk on and on about the differences between Leninism and Stalinism, but I could also tell you about certain similarities in their characteristics and methods . . . consequently, it's not possible to trace the clear line of demarcation you ask for. The seeds of some factors successively absorbed into the Stalinist system already existed when Bolshevism first appeared on the scene as a political current, that is, beginning with the Second Congress of the Russian Social Democratic Labor Party [in 1903].

Well, if we want to speak *hypothetically* of a line of demarcation . . . that is, of the point at which *quantity* began to change into

93

quality . . . I'd place it between 1928 and 1933, the period in which there occurred what Stalin called "the revolution from above," whose significance was comparable to that of the October revolution. That marked the total negation of Leninism and the transition to Stalinism.

8

The Constitution and Civil Rights

PO There's still the subject of the "hard answers given by history."
On the question of the nature of the political system that has actually emerged in the Soviet Union, there's no agreement, not even
on a definition. Some call it "state capitalism," some a "degen-
erated workers' state," and others assert that it's not even a socialist country. What do you say?

RM It's very difficult to give a concise definition of a phenomenon as
complex and contradictory from so many points of view as the Soviet state and social system. Exact definitions are the privilege of
the exact sciences while exact definitions in the social sciences are
always lacking. Unfortunately, in this country many are content to
oversimplify things. You often hear and read such statements as,
"Since full democracy doesn't exist in the USSR, neither does socialism," or "Since there are no free unions in the USSR, this isn't
socialism," or "In the USSR elections are not really free, therefore
there's no socialism," and so on. But sixty or seventy years ago,
many Marxists were saying, "Since trade and exchange still exist,
it's nonsense to talk about socialism," "If the state in a country

doesn't die out but grows stronger, it's not a socialist country or a socialist state,'' and so on.

But the question is far more complicated than that. Soviet society today is a complex mixture of real socialism and pseudo-socialism; by pseudo-socialism I mean those factors that are socialist only in their façade and terminology. If I must give an approximate definition, I'd say that the Soviet Union's system is an *authoritarian* or *statist socialism*. Experience shows us that the transition to an authentic, not deformed, socialism is a very long and laborious process that necessitates an unrelenting fight against the ossification of some social institutions and against the privileged groups which have entrenched themselves at the top as leaders of society and the state. In a country like the USSR, this struggle can go on for generations.

PO Of the groups that share in ruling the state, which ones pull the most weight in the decision-making process?

RM The basic social classes in the USSR are the workers, the peasants, and the intelligentsia. Previous Soviet constitutions stated that ours was a nation of workers and peasants, but the new one declares that "the USSR is a state of workers, peasants, and members of the intelligentsia.''

If you want to single out the forces and sectors that really run our society, then there's no doubt that the party apparatus plays the decisive role. The army that is, the ranking military leaders, don't have much to say except in moments of political crisis when there's bitter infighting at the top. That happened in 1953 after Stalin's death; in 1957 when the Presidium voted to oust Khrushchev; and again in 1964 on the eve of the October Plenum. The KGB wields tremendous power and influence, and so does the Ministry of the Interior, but to a lesser extent.

PO You refuse to deny that the USSR is a socialist nation on the grounds that public ownership is the clearest proof of its socialist character. But at the same time you maintain that to build a socialism which incorporates democratic liberties, you have to allow a certain degree of private ownership in production. Permit me a provocative question: Does this mean that total elimination of man's exploitation of man . . . that is, total socialism . . . is incompatible with freedom? And in that context, wasn't Marx wrong, and isn't the USSR too socialist to be a free country?

RM I believe that the USSR is fundamentally a socialist country, but without a developed, mature socialism. In my opinion, we're now in one of the initial phases of socialism, and the concept of "real socialism" in our specific case is more valid than the designation of a "developed socialism."

The socialist nature of our system isn't limited only to public ownership of the means of production. While we're behind the Western nations in civil rights, we've surpassed them in the area of social and economic rights. We have no unemployment or galloping inflation; the state holds the cost of prime necessities down to an extremely low level: housing, public transportation, bread, milk, potatoes, and so on. We have free medical care and free education, obligatory to the age of seventeen. The right to social security is guaranteed to the sick and the elderly. We can't deny that these benefits exist, although we can complain about the quality of our medical services and the level of education.

My vision of developed socialism doesn't extend to all freedoms, including freedom to run one's own business, but rather to civil, political, social, and economic rights. Full freedom in any business activity cannot exist under socialism, nor can one person's license to exploit another. But this certainly wouldn't prevent the growth and flowering of democracy . . . which, unfortunately, we don't have in the USSR at present.

PO Would you tell me to what extent private initiative could function within the system you envision?

RM When I speak of a degree of private initiative, I refer first of all to various forms of it in production and the services, also the freedom to found business and cooperative associations that would belong to those working in them. Marx surely couldn't have foreseen the vast expansion we have had in the services, which now begin to count more employees than the industrial sector.

In some service sectors, like air and rail transportation, individual initiative, of course, is practically unthinkable. Here state management produces the best results, although in many capitalist nations these services are entrusted to private corporations. But in some private areas initiative and small units can provide faster service and higher quality than can the gigantic and expensive state agencies—for example, in repairing domestic appliances and furniture, short-haul moving, small tailoring shops, and small boarding-houses, cafés, and restaurants, especially in vacation areas. Medicine, too, should be a free practice; it is now on paper, but it doesn't work because of crushing taxes. No one persecutes tutors who give private lessons, so why shouldn't a doctor operate just as freely? I could give you many more examples of private initiative that would be feasible both in the city and the country, and none would make inroads into the basic socialist character of Soviet society.

PO Article 17 of the new Constitution foresees a certain amount of individual initiative in small industry, agriculture, and the services involving single persons or family units. Can we interpret the sense of this article as a response to the demands we've discussed, and as the beginning of a transformation in the Soviet society?

RM In effect, Article 17 of the proposed new Constitution* augments the possibilities of personal initiative in small industries and the services—a step forward that we heartily welcome. Small artisans, tailors, innkeepers, and the like certainly can't give state-run enterprises any serious competition. On the contrary, they can provide a new impulse toward improving the big industries and achieving a higher quality of production. A small dressmaking shop, for instance, could design new models more easily and keep up with the new fashions to give its clients more satisfaction. And the big clothing manufacturers could profit from their innovations.

PO From what you've said, apparently you think that this embryonic

* The new Constitution was ratified by the Supreme Soviet on October 7, 1977, on the eve of the sixtieth anniversary of the Bolshevik revolution. The draft had been published for discussion much earlier.

98

pluralism responds more to a demand for efficiency in production than to a broader social articulation. Put differently, you see private initiative simply as an economic instrument but not yet as an opening to political pluralism. Am I right?

RM Expanding the opportunities for private initiative in industry, agriculture, and the services by no means contradicts the idea of socialism. To the contrary, it moves toward the goals of a rational socialist world by permitting some individuals to exploit potential means of increasing the community wealth. In addition, it allows people to spend their free time not only to rest but also to do things, to combine intellectual with physical work, to achieve something according to each one's inclination. But that's not all.

Neither Marxism nor Leninism appreciated the potential values of personal initiative in the realm of economics or in small, or very small, economic units. They believed that the small farmer or artisan, say, represented a form of economic activity that was dying out. But such units still exist in the capitalist world despite the rise of enormous corporations and monopolies. The majority of American farms are family-run, yet they supply a major part of America's agricultural output, and achieve very high levels of productivity, often in an integrated relationship with the giant agricultural industries, to their mutual advantage. How much more feasible integration of that kind would be in a socialist society. And that goes for all economic sectors, not just agriculture.

But you can't relate this problem to political pluralism; they are not on the same level. The political orientations of artisans or doctors who freely pursue their professions need not differ from the outlook of most ordinary Soviet citizens. On the other hand, among the workers in a big factory there may be many different opinions and different religious convictions, but that doesn't interfere in any way with the factory's output. As I've already said, political pluralism doesn't contradict socialism.

Even if Marx and Lenin interpreted the "liberal" idea and "liberalism" in a somewhat negative sense . . . in contrast to the proletariat's determination and intransigence . . . neither one ever thought that socialism by its very nature negated pluralism or

99

that everyone in a socialist system would think in the same way. Likewise, Marx never said that production figures were the *only* key to the understanding of a society. We tend to think of production reports as the foundation of society, with ideas, opinions, art, and so on, as its superstructure, but Marx and Engels wrote repeatedly that once the components of the superstructure assert themselves, they acquire a relative autonomy in their development, and they can exert a good deal of influence on the basic structure. In times nearer our own, views on the roles played by ideas and politics in general have undergone still more profound changes, assigning growing importance to the superstructures and their impact on the economy.

PO Then, if you want to appraise the potential evolution of your society, economic analysis alone isn't enough. You can't trust the more and more complex production reports to give you clues to the possible sources of change . . .

RM That's certainly not enough. In the socialist countries, political factors very often stimulate the economy by accelerating growth and mobilizing the nation's resources and reserves. But sometimes an ossified political system, a lack of control, personal political ambitions, or a misguided foreign policy will thwart economic growth. China's economy was plainly obstructed by the country's political chaos over the past two decades. In the USSR, a whole series of political reforms, if they're objective and really mature, would spur a more rapid pace in our economy.

Anyone who wants to understand Soviet society must examine it as a whole: its economic and political relations, its currents of opposition, and many other factors.

PO Going back to the new Constitution . . . it says that the dictatorship of the proletariat in the USSR is a dead issue and that the Soviet Union is now a "state of all the people." The animosities that alienated social groups are vanishing, and the whole population is joining with the proletariat in its ideological and political outlook. Judging from the philosophy of law, this seems to be a step backward vis-à-vis the preceding Constitution, which recog-

100

nized the existence of conflicting "values" and conflicts between social groups. The new Constitution apparently intends to consecrate both political and social totalitarianism, at least theoretically.

RM I don't think your viewpoint is altogether founded on fact. The first Soviet Constitution did speak of the dictatorship of the proletariat and implied that the peasantry, while allied to the proletariat, was a class of the second order. As for the intelligentsia, it fell into some sort of vague "stratum" among the other classes. The 1936 Constitution pronounced the USSR a "state of workers and peasants"; this wasn't a matter simply of words and definitions but rather of rights. When elections were held in the early years of Soviet power, one worker's vote counted as much as several peasant votes, and the party imposed a number of limitations on representatives of the intelligentsia before it accepted them into its ranks. Until recently collective farmers could not have domestic passports; this drastically restricted their freedom of movement and choice of jobs, and made it harder for them to change their place of residence for personal reasons, to have a bank account, or to register in a Moscow hotel.

Therefore, if the new Constitution mentions the power of all the people and defines the USSR as a "state of workers, peasants, and *members of the intelligentsia*," that's not a step backward as you think, but a step forward. In fact, the peasants and intelligentsia have never been granted the right to set up their own political organizations with a platform that diverged from the Communist Party's. Nowadays, while the schools of higher education often prefer applicants from working-class families, the rights of the workers, the peasants, and the intellectuals have been, at least formally, equalized.

About ten years ago, the party's Moscow City Committee summoned me to warn me against distributing some *samizdat* manuscripts. At the session, one of the committee secretaries said to me, "Don't forget that in this country we don't have a dictatorship of the intelligentsia but a dictatorship of the proletariat." Today such a statement would contradict the new Constitution.

101

PO   Of course. But when the Constitution declares that there are no antagonistic class interests because class antagonism has been wiped out, and when it goes on to say that ideological and political differences no longer exist because the whole population subscribes to the proletarian tenets on both counts, it makes me wonder . . . what political and social room is left to anyone who doesn't subscribe to those tenets.

The only answer comes from the government itself: there is only one justification for opposition—insanity; therefore dissidents are put in mental institutions.

RM   In fact, the new Constitution leaves no room for opposition. Like the one before it, the new draft concedes no right to establish political organizations outside the Soviet Communist Party, nor does it allow political minorities to formulate and defend their own views. This is the principal fault with the new Constitution and the fundamental fault in our society; it spawns all the other restrictions on our civil and political rights. I don't think that the mere existence of an opposition means guaranteed control over the activities of the groups in power; certainly, it doesn't constitute the only obstacle to the abuse of power, but it's the most consistent.

Even if we had total social homogeneity . . . which we don't have yet . . . and even if there were no conflicts of interest, there would always be differences of opinion on problems encountered in building socialism, the conduct of the Soviet Communist Party and its leaders, and the state's domestic and foreign policies. These differences provide, if not a social basis, at least a cultural basis for pluralism. I mean that even after communism is realized, there would still be situations that would engender conflicts of opinion. People can't all think in the same way—unless they stop thinking altogether.

Kautsky once said that communism means a rigid organization in production but anarchy in ideas and opinions. The word "anarchy" is not accurate, of course, but Kautsky's thought is right. Material abundance and spiritual richness must go hand-in-hand.

PO   Allow me to pursue this theme, since it's a very important one which we must clarify, first to understand what sort of socialism you and your Soviet friends want, and second, to know how to explain it correctly to those in the West who dream of building a society that's both socialist and free. Like liberal democratic constitutions, the Soviet Constitution grants many civil and political rights to its citizens. But whereas the liberal democracies proceed from the assumption that political and social competition is essential to those rights, the Soviet Constitution presupposes that socialist society knows no conflict, that it's "homogeneous." Here it seems to be at cross purposes. Don't you agree that civil and political liberties will end up as empty formalities without that competition?

RM It's not true that the new Constitution concedes no real political or civil rights to the population, but it is true that by excluding the competition you speak of, like the old Constitution, it narrows the margin considerably for exercising those rights.

Article 6 of the new draft imposes strict limits. It says:

> The leading and guiding force of Soviet society and the nucleus of its political system, of all state organizations and public organizations, is the Communist Party of the Soviet Union. The CPSU exists for the people and serves the people.
> The Communist Party, armed with Marxism-Leninism, determines the general perspectives of the development of society and the course of domestic and foreign policy of the USSR, directs the great constructive work of the Soviet people, and imparts a planned, systematic, and theoretically substantiated character to their struggle for the victory of communism.*

The article asserts *a priori* the party's "immaculate perfection" and gives legal force to its "leading role" in the country. But history bears witness to its many errors, some prolonged for years.

PO What do you suggest as an alternative?

RM You can't give a political party "the leading role" by passing a law; that must come from the moral authority it earns by specific accomplishments. Article 6 contradicts Article 2, which says that all power belongs to the people, which means that only the people

---

*The English wording is from the pamphlet *Constitution (Fundamental Law) of the Union of Soviet Socialist Republics* (Moscow: Novosti Press Agency, 1978), p. 21.

103

can give the party a mandate to exercise power and run the country. This mandate is not to be taken for granted as a permanent thing but must be renewed periodically by the will of the people; and the will of the people is best expressed through general elections, with different political parties and groups competing.

I'm not at all opposed to the party's having the leading role, but I do say that anything like Article 6 can only make the party less responsible in its actions. A clause like that belongs in the party's statutes, not in the Constitution.

PO That's Gramsci's theme. The state consists of various structures, including the public, or coercive . . . like the army and the courts . . . and the private, or hegemonic . . . parties, unions, and so on. The hegemonic concept applies to the private sphere in that it's not a juridical presupposition but the consequence of an active bid to win consensus . . . Have you read Gramsci?

RM No. Unfortunately I know very little about Gramsci, although we have a biography of him in a series on great men in history.

To return to the new Constitution . . . another inappropriate article, number 62, says: "Citizens of the USSR are obliged to safeguard the interests of the Soviet state, and to enhance its power and prestige. Defense of the Socialist Motherland is the sacred duty of every citizen of the USSR."* I can understand this duty, but why put into the Constitution a rule that binds every citizen to enhance the prestige of the state? And what does it mean, to enhance the state's prestige? That's not a matter for the courts or the Constitution. And what if I thought that the state went wrong somewhere . . . as in sending Soviet troops into Czechoslovakia? Article 62 stipulates that the citizen must automatically approve whatever is done in the name of the state. But weren't Stalin and Khrushchev leaders of the state? And weren't their actions repudiated by the highest institutions of the state?

And another thing . . . Article 62 clearly conflicts with Article 49, which provides that every Soviet citizen has the right to criti-

---

*The English wording of Articles 62, 49, and 47 is from the 1978 Novosti edition cited above.

cize shortcomings in the work of state bodies, both central and local. Doesn't that cast the shadow of doubt on their prestige? Or is Article 49 supposed to refer to organizations other than the party and to state institutions at the lower level only? It certainly doesn't say that. On the contrary, it says that in the USSR "persecution for criticism is prohibited." It's enough to befuddle the most seasoned jurist.

Well . . . Article 62 stamps every dissident action as illegal. Fortunately, the new Constitution hasn't been formally adopted yet, so no one can bring charges against me for these adverse observations, at least not under the Constitution still in force.

PO The new Article 47 grants Soviet citizens, "in accordance with the aims of building communism, . . . freedom of scientific, technical, and artistic work." This sounds like a modern rationalization for the trial of Galileo. If the discovery that the earth revolves around the sun is "in accordance with" building communism, it's a discovery. If not, then it's heresy. In practice, what does this article signify to a Soviet intellectual?

RM Well, it's a new article and good insofar as it speaks of free endeavor in science, technology, and art, but certainly not where it cancels that freedom if it doesn't contribute to building Communism. There's no logic or common sense in it. Take the greatest scientific discoveries: ideologically they were absolutely neutral, still they're utilized "in accordance with the aims" of both capitalism and socialism. When someone discovers a new galaxy today, both Soviet and American astronomers rejoice.

Some technological and scientific innovations can prove to be harmful, but the danger may not come to light for a long time, sometimes only after several decades. Therefore, introducing a *constitutional* criterion of judgment on the usefulness of scientific, technological, and artistic endeavor toward building Communism is wrong and can only bring down ridicule upon our Constitution.

Where the arts are concerned, matters are particularly delicate and complex. Who on earth, I wonder, will ever find that a work

105

by Michelangelo or Dante's *Divine Comedy* is "in accordance with the aims of building communism"?

I don't say that scientists and technologists should have unlimited freedom. For example, they shouldn't be free to damage nature or the ecology irreparably. Otherwise, only popular opinion and practice are the true criteria of creative work, not the notions of some political boss.

PO Let's take another example. The new Constitution provides for a number of representative bodies, such as unions and soviets. But if an organization is to be representative, that presupposes competition, various interests and ideas, which the Constitution rules out. In a noncompetitive society with everyone in agreement politically and ideologically, this means that good administration is enough to interpret the will of the people without ever consulting them . . .

RM That's true, unfortunately. The new Constitution allows for any number of social organizations but limits their scope of action and their autonomy. Their purpose is merely to function as "party transmission belts," as Stalin put it, to increase the party's influence in those areas of society that don't come under the direct control of party units. That is to say, every single individual, as the present Constitution stipulates, must be "guided by the party," not only ideologically but also organizationally. That's why many of our representative bodies have no power to reverse measures enacted by the central administration.

This is how the Constitution excludes politics *a priori*, at least as you understand it in the West . . . I mean ideological and political competition. Naturally, that leaves the working class, the young, and indeed all society apolitical. We have no courts of justice to affirm and defend ideas that don't conform with those of the present party leadership. Aside from contributing to the population's political apathy, this state of affairs allows arbitrary and subjective legislation to be passed and contributes to the abuse of power. Our only guarantees lie in the personal qualities of one leader or another; but we have learned from experience how feeble such guarantees can be.

9

Whither
Soviet Society?

PO There's still another discrepancy I'd like to bring up. On the issue
of a free conscience, the new Constitution recognizes the citizen's
right to profess any religion he wishes, but obliges him at the same
time to do his share toward building communism, which, of course,
is atheistic. Moral: believers are bound by duty to contribute to
their own undoing.

RM Yes. The Constitution and the party statutes are indeed guilty of
this discrepancy. Spreading atheistic propaganda is one of the
statutory obligations of every member of the Soviet Communist
Party, consequently no believer can ever join it.

　　That isn't true, however, of many Communist parties elsewhere;
not all of them exclude worship in any form. If Marxist theory
guarantees freedom of opinion, then why shouldn't Communism
guarantee freedom of religion, too? There is no such thing as absolute truth, and mankind can arrive at an absolute knowledge of the
world only through a continuing process of learning.

　　This is an elementary truth of dialectic materialism. Some may
argue, however, that even if there's no absolute truth, the gnosio-

logical conditions for *faith* in God, in the world's spiritual development, still remain. That's true, but these are personal matters,
problems for each individual conscience, and I'm positive that if
we really build Communism, it will respect freedom of conscience.

I'd like to emphasize another inconsistency in the new Constitution. The first Soviet Constitution included a clause on freedom of
religion, suggested by Lenin, which covers freedom of conscience,
the separation of church and state, the separation of school and
church, and an additional important principle: citizens were
guaranteed *freedom of religious and antireligious propaganda*.
This authorized the right to preach one's faith outside the chur-
ches, including the parents' right to impart their faith to their
children, and the right to sell religious literature. Now, I don't
want to go into the persecutions against religion and the church
under Stalin's rule, except to say that in the 1936 Constitution
nothing was mentioned about freedom of religious propaganda,
only antireligious propaganda. We see the same thing in the new
Constitution. The Communist Party disdains religion and the
church as surviving relics of past centuries that must be stamped
out.

PO On this subject, I'd like to have your opinion of a theory that's
circulating in nonconformist intellectual circles. It's this: at the
end of the last century and the beginning of this one, Russia lived
through a phase of cultural renewal often called the period of
"decadence." It was a time when Russia came its closest culturally
to Western Europe; and this period reached its height in the October revolution. But the revolution was soon transformed into a
"restoration" of traditional Russian culture, which was parochial
and intolerant. It's no coincidence that this period, when Russian
culture most nearly approximated Europe's, is officially scorned as
"decadent."

RM There might be some truth in what you say, but on the whole, this
theory is too flimsy to be valid. Clericalism and intolerance are reactionary traditions that are not unique to Russia. They are only

one direction in a country's cultural development, one which has always been opposed by another current, a lay culture seeking to expand its bonds with the West. Peter the Great, for example. At the end of the eighteenth century and the beginning of the nineteenth, Russia had assimilated a good deal from the West during the Napolenoic wars. At the end of the nineteenth century, Russia in turns began to influence European culture on a growing scale. Just think of the great composers, the writers like Tolstoy, Dostoevsky, Chekhov, Gorky, and Turgenev, scientists like Mendeleev, Pavlov, and others. After the success of the October revolution, the weight and influence of Russian cultural values continued to leave their imprint on the West. That's especially true of the 1920s in modern painting, films, and architecture. Until that point, the cultural exchanges between Russia and the West were rich and deep.

PO And under Stalin? . . .

RM I don't share the notion that the "Russian soul" took precedence over the "European spirit." A certain shift toward Russian nationalism, isolation from Western cultural and political influences, and a partial, superficial restoration of Russian traditions in many fields began under Stalin in the 1930s and continued through the 1940s. Certainly, no people should renounce everything that's precious in its history and tradition, not even in the name of world revolution. But in their great-power chauvinism, Stalin and his closest collaborators pursued other aims.

Under Khruschev, our doors were reopened to many Western values in technology, the sciences, and culture in general. This process is still going on, although far more slowly than one would wish. I think that the West, too, is absorbing something from contemporary Russian culture. It's nonsense to conceive of modern Russia and the USSR as a spiritual desert.

PO I don't deny that the Soviet people are moving ahead in spite of the ideological and governmental superstructure. But what I wonder and what I ask you is this: Where is the Soviet Union going?

109

RM With all the difficulties and obstacles in its way, Soviet civilization is still making strides in the sciences, in technology, and in culture generally.

Our literature is one of the best, and we're advancing in various important sectors of science and technology. Progress in these fields could come much faster if the bureaucratic structure of our leadership weren't holding it back. But you can't stop the impetus. I believe that this process, in spite of all the hindrances I've spoken about, is edging toward socialism.

For the moment I'd rather not discuss building communism; we're still far from it. As a historian, I don't like short- or medium-term reasoning. But if you take a span of twenty-five years and compare the USSR as it was in 1952 with the USSR today in 1977, don't you find the difference impressive in every way? Don't you agree that our science, technology, art, and literature have achieved substantial gains in this past quarter century? Even politics has gone farther ahead than one notices at first glance. Our relations with the West have improved, and I'm convinced that our progress will continue in the coming years.

Ours is not a developed socialist society, as Soviet propaganda would have us believe. We're still plagued by material shortages, including a shortage of foodstuffs. But I hope that by the year 2000 we shall not be far from that day when we can finally behold the USSR as a truly socialist nation.

PO Now we come to the essence of your thinking. You say that there are forces in the state and your society which favor transformation. You've spoken of "democrats" in the party. But how can these "potential" forces become "real" forces for change? How can a bureaucratic police state . . . which is what the Soviet Union is today . . . put reformist theory into practice?

RM When I spoke of "democrats" in the party I had in mind a relatively restricted group of functionaries, present on all levels but without organizational contacts, who took their stand against rehabilitating Stalin and favored a restructuring of the hyperbureaucratic system of party and state leadership. But these men

110

. . . and they are far fewer today than they were a decade ago
. . . are in no position to change the party by themselves or to effect a democratic conversion; to achieve that, the support of a
solid following at the party base would be indispensable. I hope
that the contradiction between the demands for technical and scientific progress and for improvements in the mass information
media, on the one hand and the government's immobility, on the
other, will stimulate such a movement.

Our daily life is riddled with any number of small crises which
centralization and planning resolve quickly; nevertheless they are
danger signals which give unmistakable evidence that our model of
socialism is aging. A development such as I have outlined could
result in relatively rapid changes of mind . . . perhaps even unexpected . . . among a great number of party members. How and
when this might come about is unpredictable because history gives
us no precedents to go by. The USSR is still exploring unknown
territory.

Being an optimist, I believe that the Soviet people await a future
that will be better, no worse, than the present. I hope, too, that
the next generation of leaders will be more sensitive to the problems posed by changing times and conditions, and thereby encourage the rise of true socialism.

PO To recapitulate . . . pluralism and competition remain the principal factors of social progress, transformation, and political
regeneration. Not even a society as closed as the Soviet Union's can
sidestep this truism; at most it can try to resist it by denying the
very dialectics of history. In short, the trend toward pluralism and
competition is an almost physiological component of modernization . . .

RM Yes. I see pluralism as a positive, indeed inevitable, phenomenon.
When I was studying philosophy at the University of Leningrad in
the late '40s, neither the instructors nor the students at the semi-
nars on dialectic materialism could hit on a solution to a riddle in
logic. On the one hand we learned that progress always comes
when you explode contradictions and surmount opposing trends,

on the other that Soviet society had already achieved total politico-moral unity, the new generating power of development. But no one could find a convincing formula to reconcile these two propositions.

Pluralism also opens another way to socialism through the variations in the different Communist parties' political and economic programs. Communist nations are vying to invent the most efficient methods of building socialism: the USSR, China, Hungary, Yugoslavia, Poland, and East Germany. Pluralism and competition can render Soviet socialism more flexible, solid, and attractive. Just as you can't bring up a robust, mentally sound child in an artificial environment, cleansed of every virus and microorganism, without constantly training the child to overcome difficulties, so is it impossible to build a Communist Party in hothouse conditions that place it apart from competition and politics.

PO   The concept of competition presupposes not only different parties and social forces but also their different ideologies. When you accept the idea of party pluralism, do you foresee nonsocialist parties . . . liberals, social democrats, and so forth?

RM   I don't identify political pluralism with the pluralism of social forces, that is, of classes. Certainly you can't say that individual artisans and people engaged privately in the services constitute a separate class, for one reason because most of them will work at their private activities only when they have time off from their other jobs. Socialist society is fundamentally homogeneous, but this doesn't exclude pluralism in ideas and political thought.

Why do you include Social Democrats among the nonsocialist parties? It is true that many Social Democratic parties, which trace their origins from the First International, led by Marx, today perform functions that the liberal parties did in the last century; but in almost all the Social Democratic parties there are strong currents on the left which favor socialism—and do not merely want to patch up the ills of capitalism. Pluralism as I see it, must permit the existence not only of different parties having socialist platforms but of nonsocialist parties too, although in a well-structured and advanced socialist society they would never represent more than a

112

negligible minority of the population, I'm sure of that. Anyway, they should have the right to express their points of view. In any society whatever, only terrorists and criminals should be outlawed.

PO You say that in a socialist society the nonsocialist forces and parties are in the minority. But in an authentic democratic situation, they should have a chance to grow into the majority and install a nonsocialist democracy. Do you envision such a possibility?

RM Well, certainly such a possibility should exist; that's what will prod any Communist or socialist regime to improve its performance and pay closer heed to the public's wishes. But then, if a nonsocialist party should win a temporary majority, it couldn't easily restore a nonsocialist system if it wanted to. That would be feasible only in the first years after a socialist victory, and then it would fall into a progressive decline. To give an example: I can't imagine how you could turn back Soviet factories, electric power plants, railroads, or any big industry to private ownership. This is an abstract hypothesis, although by rights it should exist, however theoretically.

PO Conceding this prospect, what can liberal, socialist, and democratic forces in the West do to facilitate the USSR's process of evolution and help the Soviet dissidents?

RM They could contribute considerably to the democratization of the USSR. By criticizing the defects of our system, by providing a sounding board for our dissidents and giving them moral support, the West could help us to take the first short step toward pluralism. But the West can't solve our problems; they can be solved only inside the Soviet Union itself.

To conclude our conversations, allow me to "toss a stone in your orchard," as a Russian proverb puts it. We've discussed the problems of Soviet society. But Western society is not without its own very complex and serious problems and conflicts . . . not the same as ours, of course, but difficult to iron out nonetheless. If Western democrats and socialists really want to help the Soviet Union to become a flourishing democracy, let them create such a society on their home grounds and set our people a good example.

10

Dissent in the USSR, 1978–79: Failures and Hopes

Participants in the democratic movement in the USSR, and outside observers alike, now recognize that the movement is going through a period of debilitation and even decline. The ranks of dissidents inside the country have grown thin, and fewer and fewer new ideas and new initiatives are being put forward. Of course the movement has not disappeared and, presumably, will not disappear from Soviet public life. But undeniable symptoms not only of its weakening but of a crisis in the democratic movement are evident.

Many seek a simplistic explanation for this phenomenon and find it in the intensified repression which claimed several dozen new victims among dissidents in 1977–78. But the problem is not the repression, or *not so much* the repression. Of course it's anything but safe and easy to be a dissident, to criticize fundamental aspects, or even particular aspects, of domestic and foreign policy in our country. Although an argument was made, as long ago as in the Stalin-Zhdanov era,* that

---

* Andrei Zhdanov (1896–1948), as a Politburo member and one of Stalin's closest aides, presided over a campaign of repression and intimidation against writers and artists, and "cosmopolitans" in general, from 1945 to his sudden death in 1948. The period is often referred to as *Zhdanovshchina*, the "Zhdanov times," a term with strong negative connotations.

under socialism criticism and self-criticism become a new force for progress, serious political criticism has so far failed to win any thanks from the powers that be; rather, such criticism entails serious difficulties for oppositional-minded citizens. But this was a problem familiar to the dissidents of the 1960s, and at that time the movement gained strength year after year, although government repression was much more severe in the late 1960s than it has been in the 1970s. The changes in the forms taken by the democratic movement were ways of responding to this repression. Many dissidents shifted from the tactic of drawing up petitions with hundreds of signatures (the "petition campaign" of 1967–68) to the formation of small but highly active opposition organizations.

As a rule these were legal organizations, which announced their opposition to the regime and scorned any conspiratorial methods. They openly publicized the names of their members, held press conferences, drew up and distributed various documents on the violation of human rights in the USSR. As examples of such organizations we can cite the Initiative Group for the Defense of Human Rights in the USSR (Pyotr Yakir, Viktor Krasin, Yuri Maltsev, Leonid Plyushch, Natalya Gorbanevskaya), the Human Rights Committee (Andrei Sakharov, Valery Chalidze), the Amnesty International group (Valentin Turchin, Andrei Tverdokhlebov) the Helsinki Monitoring Group (Yuri Orlov, Anatoly Shcharansky, Yelena Bonner, Lyudmilla Alekseyeva), the Russian Social Fund to Aid Political Prisoners, also known as the Solzhenitsyn Fund (Aleksandr Ginzburg), the Working Group for the Investigation of Psychiatric Abuse (Aleksandr Podrabinek, Irina Kaplun), and the Committee for the Defense of the Rights of Believers. The editorial board of the *Chronicle of Current Events* continued to exist, as did that of the *Chronicle of the Lithuanian Catholic Church*. Of course a few small conspiratorial organizations also appeared in several cities. Their aims varied, but for the most part their intent was to enlighten the public (by disseminating *samizdat* materials and books published abroad). In this chapter I will focus primarily on the legal dissident organizations. The founders and members of these organizations sought openly to assert their right to form social and political organizations. They hoped that with the expansion of détente, which reached a high point in the 1975 Helsinki conference of thirty-five heads of state and the signing of the

116

Final Act of the Helsinki accords, including an important section on the defense of political and civil rights—that in this context the creation of dissident organizations would not only be possible but would also strengthen and broaden the democratic movement. This was an illusion which nevertheless has not lost its hold on some people to this day.

My interview with the Italian journalist Pierro Ostellino, which constitutes the bulk of the present book, brings the democratic movement up to the end of 1977. I think that the arguments and ideas expressed in that interview still hold true. However, they need to be qualified and supplemented, for the situation has changed in important ways since the notorious trials of dissidents that took place in 1978 in Moscow, Kaluga,* the Baltic, and the Ukraine.

It is well known that the Western press and world opinion have paid a lot of attention to the dissident movement in the USSR for a long time. Now it has also become the object of scholarly investigation. Among the recent books on this subject that I have had the opportunity to see, I will mention one example.† In the past few years almost every book on the Soviet Union by a Western author has contained one or several chapters on the dissident movement, and in Russian-language emigré publications, the movement has become virtually the dominant theme. Understandably so, because it is through the dissident movement, with all its varied trends and viewpoints, that the many extremely important and deeply-rooted processes under way in our country can now be understood. Moreover, although the number of active dissidents at present is not large—in fact there are fewer and fewer—in a country like the USSR, such a movement is bound, sooner or later, to become a determining factor in many respects. As the contemporary American philosopher Eric Hoffer wrote, "People who are rejected and relegated to the background become raw material for the future of a nation. A stone discarded by builders becomes the cornerstone of a new world. A people

---

* The chief figure in the Kaluga trial (July 1978), Aleksandr Ginzburg, has since been released. In May 1979 he was flown to the United States along with four other Soviet political prisoners in an "exchange" for two Soviet personnel imprisoned in the United States. See footnote above on Valentyn Moroz.

† *Dissent in the USSR: Politics, Ideology, and People*, ed. Rudolf L. Tökes (Baltimore and London: Johns Hopkins University Press, 1975).

117

without its mavericks and its discontented elements is usually disciplined, decorous, peaceful, and agreeable, but without any seeds of a great future."*

As was pointed out in the interview above, a dissident movement has always existed in the Soviet Union is some form. In the 1920s the Left and Right Oppositions in the party represented only one expression of dissent, although the available literature deals most extensively with these Oppositions. There were also quite a few opposition currents and groupings within the party in the first half of the 1930s, although by then conspiratorial forms prevailed. Even Stalin's horrendous terror did not so much destroy opposition as produce new dissidents from among the loyal party members and loyal citizens against whom that terror, from 1936 to 1952, was primarily aimed. After all, didn't millions and millions of people become dissidents in the prisons and camps? And of those who survived the torments of the Gulag Archipelago, many became important members, of the new oppositional generation, twenty or twenty-five years later. Suffice it to mention people of such varying persuasions as Anatoly Levitin-Krasnov, Dmitry Dudko, Solzhenitysn, Eugenia Ginzburg, Aleksandr Voronel, Pyotr Yakir, and Mikhail Baitalsky. Various forms of opposition from the right and left existed throughout Khrushchev's "glorious decade." Some individuals and groups were roused to anger and hatred by the de-Stalinization measures Khrushchev put through; others were moved to protest by Soviet government actions in the Polish and Hungarian events of 1956 and the limitations and inconsistencies in the revelations of Stalin's crimes.

In comparison with earlier periods, the Soviet dissident movement of the 1960s took on many new features. It spread to a relatively large number of intellectuals and young people, large considering the conditions in our country, and it began to receive much more systematic and complete coverage by nearly all the Western mass media. Mainly because of this, Soviet society became far better informed about the different kinds of protest and dissent in its own midst. As early as the latter half of the 1960s, however, the dissident movement began to shrink, and

* Eric Hoffer, The True Believer (New York, 1962). (The author cites p. 40 of the Russian edition by Praeger.)

this process continued through the 1970s. It is true that a number of different international processes (which can here be lumped together under the common caption of "détente") repeatedly revived opposition in one form or another and even gave rise to brief outbursts of public protest. Nevertheless, the temporary decline of the dissident movement is a fact. In the final analysis such a decline is inevitable, because in its initial stages, almost every oppositional or revolutionary movement suffers setbacks.

The dissident movement, then, has not ended. But it has acquired qualities and features different from those of one or two years ago. How has it changed?

First, the repression of 1977–78 has unquestionably forced the dissidents—and all critics of the Soviet regime in general—to change their tactics and to orient less toward Western "publicity," which has proved to be an unreliable means of defense.

In 1975 there arose a number of specialized dissident organizations linked with world public opinion, for example, the Helsinki groups, the Amnesty group, and the Solzhenitsyn fund. To a large extent their organizers assumed that world public opinion would restrain the Soviet authorities from using repressive measures against them. But things did not turn out this way. Different forms of repression were directed not so much against "individual" dissidents as against those very organizations that had emerged.

It was my personal opinion that, under present conditions, the democratic movement would become stronger and more flexible only if it remained formally unorganized, as it had been, based on personal ties and solidarity, that it consist of informal groups of like-minded people.

Formally, the creation of dissident organizations conflicts with a flagrantly undemocratic article found in the Soviet Constitutions of both 1936 and 1977. The article requires that all public and social organizations in the USSR work under the direction of the CPSU. Thus, it is impossible in principle to have an explicitly political opposition, and any dissident organization becomes liable to criminal prosecution. But that is not the main problem. The fact is that, more often than not, the formation of organizations has narrowed rather than broadened the democratic movement, because many participants—for many different rea-

119

sons—do not wish to become members of an organization. My chief objection has always been that any dissident organization would immediately build up a substantial amount of "documentary material," including lists of addresses and card files. If this material fell into the hands of the authorities, it would provide them with a great deal of information about the activities of, and interrelationships among, the dissidents and their sympathizers, many of whom by no means desired such publicity. In addition, almost all such "legal" organizations have attracted provocateurs and other dubious types who have subsequently given testimony useful to the authorities in trials and in pretrial investigations. Suffice it to recall such names as Dobrovolsky, Lipavsky, and Petrov-Agatov.* To these names we can now add Gradoboyev, whom Aleksandr Ginzburg treated as a protégé and in whom he placed complete confidence.† Not far removed from these types are Yakir and Krasin, of whom all dissidents speak today with undisguised contempt.

Also instructive in this regard has been the functioning of the Solzhenitsyn Fund. It has undoubtedly accomplished a great deal and provided significant aid to the families of political prisoners, to prisoners who had been released, and to those in penal exile. However, insufficient pains were taken to keep the work confidential. Huge card files, with thousands of names of those actually or potentially in need, were created. Receipts were kept on transfers of funds; those who received aid directly were supposed to sign vouchers indicating the amount received; and a network of local representatives of the Fund was established. And all the records were kept, not in some out-of-the-way place but in the apartment of Ginzburg and his wife.

It is self-evident that money sent from abroad through the special

*On Aleksei Dobrovolsky, see note above p. 54. Aleksandr Petrov (pseudonym Agatov) was a longtime dissident who, in February 1977, suddenly published an open letter in the official Soviet press denouncing Aleksandr Ginzburg and other prominent dissidents for alleged criminal acts. Semyon Lipavsky published a similar letter in March 1977 denouncing Anatoly Shcharansky and other Jewish dissidents; he admitted working with the CIA himself and charged that Shcharansky and others had done likewise—a charge they deny; he apparently functioned as a KGB provocateur after entering Moscow Jewish dissident circles in 1972–73.

† Gradoboyev was a former common (not political) criminal who lived in the same town as Ginzburg and apparently helped him in the work of the Fund for Aid to Political Prisoners. At Ginzburg's trial in Kaluga in July 1978, Gradoboyev testified against him.

"gifts" department of the Soviet Bank of Foreign Trade and disbursed not in ordinary rubles but special coupon-certificates has more buying power than "ordinary" rubles because there is a special system of stores with lower-priced goods where these coupons are redeemable. But these certificates, especially in large denominations, should not have been transferred to others, because it is too easy to use the flow of certificates, as with the movement of checks, to trace the movements of people, the relations and connections among them, and the movement of literature received from abroad. All the bustling activity of the Fund took place, as it were, in plain view of the authorities, and when they lowered the boom, it was by no means only Aleksandr Ginzburg who suffered.

Of course, my objections to formal dissident organizations are tactical rather than a matter of principle. In our movement there are quite a few people who put moral considerations first and have utter contempt for questions of *tactics*. Still worse, they do not think that tactics of any kind are appropriate for the dissident movement, because any tactical approach tends in the direction of compromise, and that would violate the moral purity of the movement. Needless to say, I do not share this point of view. Only those who are striving for *effect*, rather than *effectiveness*, can take that position. We can say with certainty that if Solzhenitysn had not taken the strictest precautions in writing *Gulag Archipelago*; if instead, he had announced the formation of some Working Group to Investigate the Crimes of the Communist Party, which he hates so much, he would never have been able to accomplish that task. Why, then, did he suppose he would be allowed to send royalty monies earned from the sales of *Gulag Archipelago* into the USSR for distribution to those whom the Soviet authorities, often without justification, consider their enemies?

The situation in which our society finds itself at present is such that the most important instrument for change remains the truthful word, that is, the production and dissemination of truthful works of art, scholarship, and political commentary, as well as accurate documentation of various kinds. Usually such works can be written or compiled without any formal organization.

As for the distribution of truthful information, we have gone backward rather than forward in the 1970s. *Samizdat*, that is, the massive,

121

uncontrolled circulation of manuscript copies of oppositional works, which began with so much promise, has virtually ceased to exist. Today there are many more *samizdat* works than in the 1960s, if we include the numerous books by Soviet and emigré Russian authors published in the West in the 1970s. But unfortunately the Russian books published abroad reach the USSR in insignificant numbers—dozens and even hundreds of times fewer than the celebrated circulation of *samizdat* in the 1960s.

Of course experiments in organizing various types of dissident groups should continue. For example, I supported the initiative of a group of Muscovites and Lithuanians in early 1979 when they formed a temporary public organization, Election -79, to nominate their own independent candidates for elections to the Supreme Soviet of the USSR. The by-laws of this organization were drawn up to conform fully to existing Soviet law. Its aims did not conflict in any way with the official "Regulations for Elections to the Supreme Soviet," many of whose clauses are quite democratic but simply not observed in practice by the authorities.

In the 1960s it seemed to many dissidents that changes in our internal structure could occur rather quickly, that a few years of struggle and reform would be enough to transform the Soviet Union into a land of flourishing democracy. But twelve or thirteen years have passed. As a world power the Soviet Union is undoubtedly mightier in military and industrial respects. Much less progress has been observed in agriculture over these years. And we have seen even less progress in the expansion of democratic liberties, tolerance of dissenters, reduction of censorship, and so on. As a result many dissidents have turned from optimists into pessimists. They declare that the Soviet regime is incapable of any political evolution and will become more and more harshly repressive. Thus, after a few clashes with the authorities, many dissidents hasten to leave the country, especially since freedom to emigrate both for Jews and people of other nationalities has been greatly expanded in the 1970s—despite various continued restrictions. At present the number of former Soviet dissidents living abroad (the so-called third emigration) is much greater than the number of dissidents remaining in the USSR. I am not about to condemn these people, as Solzhenitsyn and Shafarevich do. But in my opinion, not all of them by any means had really solid reasons for emigrating.

122

There is an old but rather depressing aphorism on the difference between optimism and pessimism. "A pessimist says that things are bound to get worse; an optimist says they couldn't possibly get worse." This clever bit of irony doesn't really apply to the situation in the USSR, however. Things could get worse or they could get better; everything depends on the circumstances and what people do.

In late 1977 the Italian newspaper *Corriero della Sera* arranged an open debate in its Moscow offices between myself and Professor Aleksandr Zinoviev, author of *The Yawning Heights*. Zinoviev at once identified himself as a pessimist, by saying:

> Such aspects of Western civilization as democracy and liberalism are not at all necessary for the normal existence of Soviet society. . . . The majority of the Soviet population has no use whatsoever for those things, and the privileged layers view them as threats to their security. Our society is altogether different from Western society. It produces a different type of person, who is satisfied by different kinds of values. . . . With time, people here will entirely cease to understand what individual freedom means in the Western sense. . . . For the greater part of society, the reality, that is, today's "actually existing socialism" is a desirable one. (*Corriero della Sera* [Milan], Literary Supplement, No. 1, Nov. 5, 1977)

I disagreed with Zinoviev, of course. Our social system does produce a type of person different in many respects from the type produced by Western social systems. In some respects this type is better and in some respects worse. Soviet citizens have never lived under genuine democracy and therefore don't always clearly understand democratic values. But it isn't true that all they want is an increase in the available material goods, or (speaking of the "elite") an increase in privileges and power. It is not hard to show that Soviet citizens are concerned about the expansion of their democratic rights and liberties. It can be shown as well that among the privileged not everyone by far is totally caught up in the chase after privileges and power. In the economic and political evolution of a country like the USSR periods of economic and political stagnation can occur, even periods of regression, but no social and political impasse will last indefinitely. Change is not only possible in our country, it is inevitable—although there could be change for the worse as well as for the better.

There continue to be quite a few different viewpoints among dissidents

123

today on the *nature* and *substance* of the changes they consider desirable. The main trends in social thought in this regard have not altered much since the 1960s. The only unexpected development has been the vigorous declaration by Solzhenitsyn and his not very numerous followers in favor of the creation of an authoritarian theocratic state in Russia, in which people would get along with a minimum of necessities and would perfect themselves morally and spiritually on the basis of the Russian Orthodox religion. But it is quite obvious that what has recently happened in Iran could not happen in modern Russia. The Soviet Union is not Iran and Solzhenitsyn is no Khomeini. This certainly doesn't imply, incidentally, that the legal rights of religious believers of every faith should not be respected in our country. And the more moderate religious opposition is fighting to have such rights guaranteed.

After the Solzhenitsyn tendency, the second major current in Soviet oppositional thought is still the "liberal" or "legalist" movement, whose most outstanding representative is Academician Sakharov. This movement continues to focus its efforts on defending such basic human rights as freedom of speech, freedom of information, freedom to emigrate, and the rights of political minorities to formulate and advocate their views. This movement has long advocated an amnesty for all political prisoners and tries to bring the weight of Western public opinion to bear on behalf of "prisoners of conscience" who have been arrested or are in confinement.

The various national movements also persist, although on a smaller scale. Their demands range from the right to return to their ancestral homeland (the Crimean Tatars) and the expansion of national autonomy to secession from the USSR by one or another of its constituent republics.*

The movement for "socialism with a human face" (a term borrowed from the Czechoslovak reformers) also continues to exist. This is an un-

---

* An example of persisting national dissent was a joint call for self-determination for Latvia, Lithuania, and Estonia issued by forty-five citizens of those republics to foreign journalists in Moscow on August 24, 1979. Their republics, they argued, had been annexed illegally in 1940 as a result of secret protocols to the Nazi-Soviet nonaggression pact signed on August 24, 1939. A separate statement by prominent Moscow dissidents, including Sakharov and members of the Helsinki Watch Group, expressed support for the Baltic dissidents' appeal.

fortunate name because what must be changed is not just the face, not just the façade of the colossal structure of "actually existing" socialism. What is hidden behind that façade must also be reconstructed. Above all, socialism must be fused with democracy in the fullest sense. In this respect the movement for "a human socialism" encompasses all the rational aspects of the other social movements. Because true socialist democracy must provide for freedom of speech and of the press, freedom for political minorities, and it must emphatically repudiate all violence toward dissenters, respect religious rights, and eliminate all artificial obstacles for religious groups. Of course all national groups in the USSR should have the opportunity to increase their cultural, political, and economic autonomy and to freely decide their own national problems, if this does not conflict with the valid interests of other nations and nationalities inhabiting the country. A return to capitalism in the USSR is no longer possible, although we could apply certain economic devices that have justified themselves completely in a number of socialist, as well as capitalist, countries (for example, the revival of individual, cooperative, and in some isolated cases privately-owned enterprise in petty commodity production and the services).

The differences among the dissidents involve not only the nature and substance of desirable changes but also the *methods* for achieving them. Only a few isolated individuals in the USSR and among the emigrés propose that we prepare for some sort of new revolution, not just Solzhenitsyn's moral revolution but a political revolution, one using violence (as advocated by Dmitry Panin). In fact, all the main currents or trends of social thought in the USSR speak emphatically in favor of non-violent methods, of reforms. There has been so much violence in our country in the twentieth century that a solid dislike of violent methods has emerged at all levels of the population. Many dissidents, aware of the limited effect they themselves have had and the absence of any mass movement favoring reform, place their hopes on outside pressure, by which we mean not only the pressure of Western public opinion but also pressure from various government institutions, for example, the U.S. Congress and the White House. Calls are made for an end to trade between the West and the USSR, for boycotting all forms of scientific and cultural exchange, and for non-participation in the 1980 Olympics in

125

Moscow. Some Soviet emigrés, along with certain Western politicians, have even suggested suspension of the strategic arms limitation talks (SALT).

To accept these proposals would be to open a new round in the Cold War between East and West, which would do appreciable harm not only to the East but to the West as well and would lead to results directly opposite to those intended. The support of public opinion, above all, the press in the Western countries, is very important for all currents in the Soviet democratic movement. But rational moderation must be observed in all things. Ultimately any serious changes in a country like the USSR will depend not so much on pressure from outside as on internal processes, including action and initiatives by "those at the top."

In the history of every major country, including the United States, Germany, Japan, England, and Russia, many very important reforms, sometimes even violent revolutions, have occurred through a combination of pressure "from below" and initiatives (or concessions) "from above." Violent revolutions tend to occur only when the ruling classes in a country prove to be too conservative and fail to pay attention to the growing discontent of the people and their own growing weaknesses. In the 1970s Portugal, Iran, and Afghanistan were countries that proved unable to avoid violent revolution, although they have not all (so far) had such bloody civil wars as occurred in Angola, South Vietnam, Ethiopia, and Kampuchea. But of course the kind of peaceful democratic changes that have occurred in Greece and Spain are preferable by far. After all, were not such famous reformers as Alexander II, Bismarck, Franklin D. Roosevelt, Khrushchev, and de Gaulle the heads of their governments? More such examples could be given.

I do not mean to imply that democratization could be like "charity" granted to the people by the ruling circles without any effort on the people's part. A struggle is being waged and the dissidents are not playing the least important role in it. But the struggle has not yet been effective enough to prompt the authorities to make serious concessions.

Until recently almost all dissidents shared my hopes for the possibility of intelligent initiatives "from above." This partly explains the mass "petition campaign" that began in 1966–67 and continued more or less into the mid-1970s. Letters and appeals to the Soviet leaders were written by hundreds of people, including the most prominent dissidents as well as many prominent writers, scientists, artists, and economic officials who were not dissidents at all. In fact, in the late 1960s a special term, "petition signers" (*podpisanty*), was invented for this common type. Even Solzhenitsyn, for all his fury against the authorities, wrote his famous 1973 *Letter to the Soviet Leaders,* expressing the hope, "faint but not nonexistent," that his proposals would be considered. I do not think the entire "petition campaign" proved useless. It prevented the partial rehabilitation of Stalin and contributed to improving the situation for certain political prisoners. But it would have been naïve to expect that petitions alone would have a great impact.

But are there, among the ruling powers in our country, the human forces capable of carrying out the changes that are urgently needed? I believe there are, although they are not in the majority. It would be a great error to think that someone who still works "within the system" and holds an important position within it is therefore incapable of doing anything to promote the liberalization and democratization of the system. An honest engineer, scientist, factory manager, director of a scientific institute, stage director, or an ordinary industrial worker, an official in the party apparatus, or an honest military officer—all such types are able in many cases to do far more good for the progressive and democratic development of our society when they are working "within the system" than when they find themselves outside it. Of course this requires not only honesty and courage but certain definite compromises. However, there is a fundamental difference between the notion of "compromise" and that of "unprincipled behavior."

I will not give many examples. But in my opinion, in the 1960s, the work of such people as Aleksandr Tvardovsky as editor-in-chief of *Novy Mir,* of B. L. Astaurov as head of a major biological research center, of Academician Igor Tamm, of the film director Mikhail Romm, and the writer Konstantin Paustovsky did no less good, and perhaps did more to awaken and push forward the positive self-awareness of our society, than many dissidents of that decade who were widely publicized in the Western press. In exactly the same way Solzhenitsyn's *One Day in the Life of Ivan Denisovich,* published in the USSR with the approval of the Presidium of the party's Central Committee, had a greater effect on the development of Soviet society and literature than later works of his, which were undoubtedly much more radical but which did not reach as broad a Soviet readership. We can see, therefore, how unjust and inappropriate it was for former Major General Pyotr Grigorenko to call Tvardovsky a "coward" the very first time he met him simply because Tvardovsky refused to sign one of the appeals Grigorenko and his friends had drawn up.

Of course the higher we go in the party and government hierarchy the fewer people of Tvardovsky's type we meet. However, even here the situation is not as hopeless as some think, as shown not just by the example of the party's Twentieth Congress, to which Solzhenitsyn refers in his *Letter to the Leaders*. There is also Azerbaijan and Georgia, where decadence and corruption reached shocking proportions in the 1950s and 1960s. In the 1970s steps have been taken precisely "from above" to improve the situation decisively, which shows that the possibility of combining pressure "from below" with initiatives from above is by no means "nonexistent."

In this I do not wish to belittle the movement consisting of dissidents "outside the system." As small as their numbers are, their movement remains an important catalyst for the kinds of change that can take place within the Soviet system. However, as we argue and work for change, we should keep in mind all the factors contributing to it—the dissident movement, the work of people "within the system," the role of the economy, which becomes more and more difficult to regulate and manage as it grows larger and more complex, the pressure of Western public opinion, and that indefinable but important factor that can be called the spirit of the times.

On more than one occasion in the past I have had to speak against the imposition of some "moral and political unity" upon the Soviet dissident movement, against its subordination to any one "unimpeachable authority." A movement whose main demands are freedom of speech and pluralism cannot fail to encourage debate and discussion within its own ranks. But in periods of decline such debates have a tendency to turn into unprincipled personal squabbles and are often accompanied by various slanderous charges and countercharges. As far as one can tell from the emigré press, this kind of atmosphere is especially prevalent now in emigré circles.

128

Of course there were fundamental differences among the various currents in the dissident movement in the 1960s, and discussion and debate intensified in the first half of the 1970s. This is natural, because there always comes a time when emotional protest has to give way to more comprehensive statements of political, social, religious, ethical, and cultural program and doctrine. But when a social movement experiences a downturn, disagreements over such matters will frequently degenerate into petty disputes, which are encouraged and often inspired by organizations having an interest in such dissension. For example, in recent months there has been an extraordinary increase in various types of anonymous letters containing the vilest slander and obscenity, portraying the private lives of certain dissidents in the most perverted way. Special books have appeared, such as one by a Czech journalist Tomas Rezac entitled *The Spiral of Solzhenitsyn's Betrayals*, in an edition by Moscow's Progress Publishers for circulation in official circles only. The Foreword to this book expresses "sincere gratitude" to the dissident Soviet writer Lev Kopelev, who for many years was in the same labor camp as Solzhenitsyn. But Kopelev never made, either verbally or in writing, a single one of the biting comments attributed to him concerning Solzhenitsyn's "lack of talent." Nor did he ever give interviews to the journalists who are named in the book and whose "interviews" are quoted there. It is true, of course, that Kopelev has criticized Solzhenitsyn's political views and program, both in published writings and in private conversations, but those are political disagreements not scurrilous personal insults.

Such techniques of moral blackmail are supplemented by repression against those dissidents, of all persuasions, whom the authorities apparently regard as incorrigible. Some are forcibly expelled from the country, for example, the prominent Soviet scholar Aleksander Zinoviev, author of the sharply satirical *Yawning Heights*. Zinoviev had already been subjected to restrictions and persecution. In 1977 he was stripped of his academic titles and even the military honors he earned for valor in the war against Nazi Germany. When he asked for permission to make a trip abroad in response to an invitation to teach at a university, a year went by without any answer. Then in the summer of 1978 he was suddenly given ten days in which to leave for West Germany, and shortly after he arrived he was deprived of his Soviet citizenship.

129

In the spring and summer of 1978 a number of well-known dissidents were brought to trial and sentenced to long terms in prison or internal exile, among them Yuri Orlov, Aleksandr Ginzburg, Anatoly Shcharansky, and about twenty others in different Soviet cities and republics. These trials have been reported in sufficient detail in the Western press. Such political trials deserve emphatic condemnation, and so does the way in which they are conducted. Foreign correspondents were not allowed to attend the trials, but neither were many relatives and friends of the defendants, who had far more reason to be there than the specially selected public which filled the courtrooms. The question inevitably arises: If the charges against Orlov, Ginzburg, and the others are fully justified and easily proved, how explain the fact that these trials were for all practical purposes closed to the public? In addition, the Soviet press limited its coverage of the trials to such brief articles that no thoughtful reader would be able to understand why the defendants were sentenced to such long terms.

I, too, have been the object of malicious slander several times in the last few years. There are *samizdat* materials from which I learned, variously, that I am a leader of a secret organization of Moscow "Jew Masons" and a member of a "Moscow Zionist committee." A number of articles in the emigré press have discussed the "problem" of why, although I have published so many books and articles abroad, I have not been arrested. Abdurakhman Avtorkhanov wrote in the December 14, 1978, issue of the newspaper *Russkaya Mysl* (Russian Thought; published in Paris) that I used the "secret archives of the KGB" in writing my books that "the secret inner thoughts (*samye sokrovennye dumy*) of the Communist Party Central Committee and the KGB" are expressed in my books and articles. But I have never worked in government archives, whether open or "closed." On the contrary, my own archives of scholarly research material have been almost entirely confiscated from my home for the second time during searches carried out by the KGB and the Moscow procuracy.

The situation that exists among the emigrés and in dissident circles within the USSR is often affected by the personal qualities of those who find themselves in opposition to the regime. I am frequently asked, "How and why do people become dissidents in the USSR?" As I have said, discontent, disagreement, and opposition are features found in any society and any country. Of course, to be a dissident in the USSR is to bring many difficulties and deprivations upon oneself. Therefore dissatisfaction with the regime or certain aspects of it does not very often develop into open and active opposition. Nevertheless many do take this step, for various reasons. In a number of cases the influence of relatives and friends plays the chief role. Quite a few people have become dissidents as a result of the powerful emotional shock of injustice done to them or those close to them. People with a sharp sense of national identity, who feel that their national group is a victim of discrimination, also become dissidents. So do those with a heightened sense of social conscience, who suddenly become aware of the injustice and lawlessness that has gone on and still goes on in our country. For example, literature about the crimes of the Stalin regime, the concentration camps, the torture, arbitrary rule, and lawless violence, has made dissidents of quite a few comparatively young people.

But it would be wrong to think that dissidents are always highly decent people with a refined sense of justice. Vladimir Maksimov was unfortunately right in part when he said that it is often embittered incompetents who become dissidents. They are unable to advance in their chosen sphere of work, not because of conflicts with the reigning ideology, but from lack of ability. But they do not wish to admit this even to themselves. It is simpler and easier to blame society, the "bosses," the censorship, and the political situation in the country in general for their failures. I remember Tvardovsky reading the stenographic text of a bitter speech by a writer against the arbitrary acts of the censors and saying with a touch of scorn: "Much of what he says is certainly true. But why does he complain that the censors held up one of his works? I would never have published that in my magazine even if all the censors had begged me to."

In the dissident movement there are people who "come for the glory," as Maksimov put it, that is out of vanity, and not because of a sharpened sense of social justice. One might wonder what kind of glory-seeking is possible when dissidents can expect only persecution, dismissal from their jobs, or confinement in penal exile, a labor camp, or even a psychiatric hospital. But that is their fate only *inside* the Soviet Union.

131

On the other side of the border, articles and essays are written about the dissidents, their statements are quoted in the press, their photographs appear in magazines. The American journalist Robert Kaiser wrote the following in one of his analytical articles about the Soviet dissidents: "the modern generation of Soviet dissidents has received an extraordinary amount of attention in the West. The popular news media have turned a few of them into something more like movie stars than political outcasts."

Kaiser tried to justify the great attention the West pays to Soviet dissidents.

> One could argue that the world should concentrate on the mainstream of Soviet life and pay less attention to these aberrational figures, so appealing to Westerners because they share the values we claim to respect. Certainly the popular media in the West have distorted the current Soviet scene by concentrating on the dissidents, but that is no argument for ignoring them. Sakharov and Solzhenitsyn are probably no less representative of their time in Russian history than Pushkin and Tolstoi were of theirs. (*Problems of Communism*, January–February 1976, p. 92)

It is superfluous to comment on how important the attention of the Western press and other mass media is to Soviet dissidents. And the publicity is fully deserved in most cases. But some who are overly hungry for fame are inspired to "become dissidents" mainly for the sake of media coverage. Fame and glory become more important to them than the interests of the cause. They want their every step as dissidents to be recorded by the foreign press; they constantly seek out Western correspondents and are even willing to suffer for the sake of *pablisiti* [a new loan-word in Russian]. Thus, a totally false set of values has begun to spread among a certain group of Soviet dissidents. There is a tendency to judge people not by how much they have done for the movement but how many times they have been questioned or searched, how many years they have spent in prison, camp, exile, or psychiatric hospitals, or even how many times they have been written up in the foreign press or mentioned in foreign radio broadcasts. Just as the theatrical and film worlds produce their own kind of Bohemia, their hangers-on, a kind of Bohemian milieu has gradually grown up around the dissidents, and this merely detracts from the serious aims and purposes of the democratic movement.

132

I have mentioned only the most important factors that in my opinion have affected the nature, forms, and goals of the dissident movement in the past year or two. Some of the most perceptive Soviet intellectuals, who follow the evolution of the movement closely although they are not directly active in it, have noticed these problems. As an example, I take the liberty of quoting at length from an interesting letter I recently received. I call it tentatively "A Letter from the Provinces," and for obvious reasons I leave out the author's name.

The dissident movement has been engaged for ten years or so in the defense of individual rights that have been trampled underfoot: the right to express one's opinion and one's free will. There is no denying the importance of this. In a certain sense the right to express oneself freely, freedom of criticism, and the expression of one's free will are the key to everything. If the conditions for freedom of speech are created, all the other freedoms will be restored as a matter of course. A society that criticizes itself will prove capable of development, of rapidly reviving what had been killed; and there will be ample scope for everything fresh and new.

Violations of rights in many areas of economic and social life and many injustices will disappear of their own accord—just through the free exchange of opinions. But in practice almost all attempts at free expression have been harshly suppressed and many brave people who have tried to put into practice the freedoms proclaimed by the Constitution have been punished in one way or another. The movement for human rights itself has more and more been drawn by the logic of events down the road of fighting to free its own victimized members or to improve their lot. Just as the members of the People's Will* in their day imperceptibly became involved in self-justifying acts of revenge, so now many dissidents have gradually turned the struggle for human rights into a struggle, granted also a very noble one, for the freedom of their comrades, for the right to leave the country, for easing the conditions in the labor camps, and so on.

Even Sakharov, who started out with very wide-ranging views on the fate of civilization, our country and the world, has been caught in the whirlpool of the struggle for the rights of persecuted dissidents and has noticeably narrowed his horizons. He is almost completely bogged down in interceding in an endless series of court cases. Less prominent people have at times lost their heads. Caught up in the heat of the struggle, they try to come to the aid of "their own people" with emergency declarations and protests that re-

---

* The People's Will (*Narodnaya Volya*) was the conspiratorial organization of Russian *Narodiniks* (populists), found in 1879, which after a number of attempts actually assassinated Tsar Alexander II in 1881. The leaders were captured and executed and in the reaction that ensued the organization was destroyed.

verberate loudly overseas. The dissident movement is now suffering the illness of every movement that is hemmed in on all sides; it suffers not only from external persecution but also from its own illusions, self-delusion, and sectarian emotions—inevitable in an artificially isolated milieu of people under persecution.

Those larger mass movements that are aligned with the dissident intelligentsia but which are inspired by national or religious aims also have rather narrowly specific features. It is understandable that the Jews and Volga Germans should demand the right to emigrate and that the Crimean Tatars demand the right to return to their native region. But these legitimate demands do not have a nationwide appeal in such a giant country as ours with a predominantly Russian population. The same can be said of the religious movements, which are mainly concerned with the defense of particular sects and hardly deal with questions concerning the Russian Orthodox Church as a whole. Without denying the legitimacy of these particular rights and interests, I nevertheless think that on the level of the democratic movement in the USSR as a whole there has been a certain shift toward a narrow in-group existence, toward sectarianism, and the self-defense of the rebel intelligentsia. . . .

To a certain extent of course this process is inevitable. The pressure of the authorities on all forms of thought, the intimidation and deception of the masses, have pushed the country far back from the moods of social renewal and moral rebirth which prevailed up to the mid-1960s. The participants in the democratic movement were formed back then, no matter how far they have now departed from their former views. They are the products of *that* epoch, they rode the crest of *that* wave, and it is not evident that many people from later generations have joined them.

But time has passed. The democratic movement has become increasingly illegitimate in the eyes of the authorities. The ideas and aims of the participants have narrowed down to liberal ones only, focusing on the problem of rights for the members and the struggle for rights. Meanwhile a vast number of difficult problems affecting the life of the country as a whole have come to the fore. Agriculture is in a state of permanent crisis. The peasant's feeling of being the master of the land has been totally destroyed, and the planned transition to an industrially based agriculture has proven premature. The food situation is growing worse, even in the capital, never mind the provinces. An enormous number of industrial units operate inefficiently. Capital construction is poorly managed and results in the irrational waste of vast resources. In trade there are shortages and theft. In finance there is chronic inflation. Among the people there is disillusion, apathy, avoidance of work, drunkenness. In the government there is stagnation, lack of any bold decision-making, fear of responsibility at every level, self-deception and outright fraud. . . .

Our dissidents scarcely notice all this, caught up as they are in the struggle for human rights. But here too there is an ocean of illegality in the han-

134

dling of criminal and civil cases, especially cases involving juveniles. Therefore the not so numerous "political" cases seem like a small matter compared to the injustices committed every day. But can we really ignore the fact that the most important social and civil rights, affecting the lives of all the people, their material conditions, opportunities for education, legal defense, and so on, are often vitiated and reduced to the bare minimum? . . .

There is no denying that the democratization of society is related to its liberalization. But the struggle for human rights will succeed only if the dissidents broaden their horizons and move from an exclusive preoccupation with the persecution of dissidents to a concern with the life and rights of the worker from Tula, the collective farmer from the Vologda region, the librarian from Tetyushi and the vocational-school student in Podolsk.

I subscribe wholeheartedly to the views of my correspondent.

What then are the prospects for the dissident movement at present? It is obvious that the authorities cannot totally eliminate the movement through persecution, arrests, internal exile, and expulsion from the country, although a reduction in the size of the movement is evident. Attempts are plainly being made to cut off the "incorrigibles" from their social base, that is, the creative intelligentsia. In addition to the "tightening of the screws" in certain areas, above all in politics, a certain "liberalization" is simultaneously being permitted, in some spheres of culture and the arts. Many cultural figures who have reputations as "liberals" or at least as free-thinking and independent people have been given far greater opportunity than before to publish their writings, to produce plays and films, and to write scholarly works.*

---

* In January 1979, in the apparent hope that the "liberalization" could be carried further, a group of twenty-three Soviet writers, including prominent members of the official Writers Union, submitted the "almanac" *Metropol* (a literary anthology they themselves had compiled and edited) and asked that the authorities publish it as is, without censorship. (Some of the manuscripts had circulated in *samizdat*; others had been rejected by editors over the years on the grounds that they would not pass the censors.) None of the prose, poetry, drama, and cultural commentary is explicitly political, and the contributors are not dissidents in the sense of being active political opponents of the Soviet system. The introduction to *Metropol* states its editors' belief that "the author alone is responsible for his work," i.e., not the censor.

The official reaction, contrary to hopes, was quite negative. Not only did the Writers Union leadership refuse to publish the anthology, reprisals were also taken against several contributors. A film written by one was withdrawn; a broadcast by another canceled; and two had their membership in the Writers Union "suspended." In response, six contributors threatened to resign unless their colleagues were reinstated. In December it became clear that the two would not be reinstated, at which point Vasily Aksyonov and two others resigned. The six included a number of prominent Soviet writers.

135

The conflict over the anthology continued within literary circles for most of the year. In September Felix Kuznetsov, chairman of the Moscow branch of the Soviet Writers Union, published a letter to American writers who had protested in behalf of *Metropol*'s contributors. Kuznetsov called attention to several cases in mid-1979 in which works by *Metropol* authors had been published in the official press. This seemed to mark a retreat from the policy of reprisals followed early in the year. In October there were reports that retaliatory action by the authorities would be stopped altogether and the two ousted writers would be restored to membership in the writers' organization in November.

The end result was perhaps some greater leeway for avant-garde writing and writers within Soviet literature, although the attempt to publish without censorship did not succeed. The anthology has apparently not circulated widely in its manuscript form in the USSR. But a Russian edition was published in the United States and an English-language edition is forthcoming.

Regardless of the authorities' intentions, it is a positive development. But these "indulgences" from above can have only a temporary effect as long as the basic problems of the peoples of the Soviet Union remain unsolved. The weakened movement sooner or later will recover and gain new strength. This is inevitable because, without a dissident movement, it will be impossible to solve the most important and complex problems of public life in a country like the USSR.

All reasonable people are opposed to senseless terrorism and violence. But a reasonable opposition is necessary in any well-organized society. This is especially true in highly complex modern societies, in which any important decision requires free debate and consideration of different points of views and independent opinions. Human history has not yet worked out a better way for a society to control the activities of government authorities—or any form of authority, be it a party, a trade union, or an economic institution. Free criticism and the right of opposition are the only way.

A country that tries to suppress and destroy any and all opposition impoverishes itself in every respect. The English philosopher and statesman John Stuart Mill wrote:

> Even in a time when reason has been enslaved there have been and can again be great thinkers; but in a time of mental servitude there never was

and cannot be an intellectually advanced people. If such a people achieved at one time a certain measure of rational development, it was only because it was, if only for a time, free from the fear of holding heretical views. But whenever principles are above criticism, and discussion of the greatest questions of human life is considered closed, it is impossible to hope that such intellectual activities as distinguished certain historical epochs, could one day develop.

The entire course of human history demonstrates the correctness of this view.

Nikolai Sokolov, a nineteenth-century Russian democrat and journalist, wrote in his little-known book *Outcasts* that among the sound and vital principles of the day were not only material necessities but also people's faith and the moral world of society. These principles, he said, cannot be endangered by any criticism and do not need to be defended by force and violence. Persecution of the negative elements who criticize society, Sokolov stressed, is evidence not of the strength but of the weakness of a society that has ceased to believe in its own rightness, morality, and worth.

We are convinced that socialism, although it can take different forms under different conditions, is a vital doctrine, neither obsolete nor moribund. But socialism has not been perfected anywhere, in theory or in practice. And for that reason the persecution of dissenters is doubly unacceptable and objectionable in socialist countries.

Dissent and opposition will inevitably exist in the Soviet Union if only because major problems affecting the life of our society have not yet been solved. And if there is an attempt to destroy the legal and loyal opposition by violence or in any other way, it will revive in the future in any case. But then it may take forms that really will be dangerous for society.

The weakening and decline of the dissident movement in recent years is an undeniable fact. But for me it is also undeniable that the decline is only temporary. In its goals and aims the democratic movement of the 1970s sprang from the moods of social renewal and moral regeneration that prevailed up to the mid-1960s, as my correspondent suggested. But the pressure of the authorities, emigration from the country, natural weariness, the lack of any clear-cut accomplishments, and gradual but by no means progressive shifts of public mood—all this has largely

137

shaped the present dissident movement, with too few people from newer generations joining over the last ten years.*

But the problems that gave rise in the mid-1960s to the stage of the movement now reaching its culmination have not disappeared. Some of those problems have now grown even more challenging and difficult. A number of new problems have also emerged. In all likelihood they will help to shape public attitudes in the 1980s. One need not be a prophet to say that the 1980s will bring a new generation of leaders to our country. I am certain that a new generation of dissidents will also appear. It is impossible to foresee exactly what kind of people will decisively determine the features of the Soviet leadership and opposition in the 1980s. But perhaps in the coming decade the dialogue between government and opposition which was unthinkable over the past twenty years will at last become a possibility.

---

* Late in 1978 there was an indication, at least in Leningrad, of significant stirring among some in the young generation. Approximately two hundred young people, mostly students, demonstrated in that city on Constitution Day, December 5, 1978. The protest was called by people in their teens and twenties who identified themselves as a "left opposition" (according to the samizdat journal Chronicle of Current Events, No. 51, December 1978). They were protesting the arrests in October 1978 of Aleksandr Skobov and Arkady Tsurkov, leading figures in "new left" circles which had been active in Leningrad since 1976. The group had begun a discussion journal, Perspectives, in the spring of 1978. At the time of the arrests, the third issue was being prepared and there were plans for a conference—apparently with similar groups from Moscow, Gorky, and possibly other cities. Skobov, a fourth-year history student at Leningrad University, had rented an apartment and made it available as a "commune" where young people from many parts of the USSR were free to stay and engage in free-wheeling discussions on politics, philosophy, culture, and art, exchange samizdat literature, and consult a library of hard-to-find books. The "commune" lasted for a year and a half until it was closed down by police in September 1978.

In April 1979, Skobov was sentenced to compulsory treatment in a psychiatric hospital and Tsurkov to five years in a labor camp and two years internal exile.

Postscript

Dissent in the USSR, 1980

Human footprints, the tracks of dogs and crows dot the dry snow, like powdered glass, with startling precision. The temperature is 18° below zero. The time is almost noon, yet this nondescript courtyard on the far periphery of Moscow is deserted; no one loiters in the gelid air, which penetrates your overcoat and insinuates itself under your woolen sweater. An automobile, mounted on bricks where its wheels should be, is wintering in the open under a shell of snow, which protects it both from the cold and from thieves given to stealing windshield wipers and rear-view mirrors. At the entrance to the apartment building stands a shiny black sedan; two men sitting inside have left the motor running. The car bears a "Mok" license plate, one of those, people whisper,

While this book was in press, Roy Medvedev gave a further interview on dissent in the USSR to Vittorio Zucconi of the *Corrière della Séra*, Milan, which appeared February 4, 1980.

139

assigned to the Ceki secret police. So . . . they have come. On the fifth floor of the building lives Roy Aleksandrovic Medvedev, historian, political analyst, intellectual, a "free dog" of the dissident movement, and a prime candidate for imminent arrest.

To talk with a dissident at the pre-Olympic moment is like peering down into an abyss or venturing into the antechamber of a criminal court. The man who opens the door to me is fifty-four years old; his hair is white, and he wears a shetland sweater over ill-fitting jeans, a gift. They say that he is one of the few who know how to keep afloat, to hang on with powerful fingers. They say, too, that he is "sly." I don't know what it means to be "sly" in the USSR, but in any event, Roy Medvedev is indeed a singular type.

I'm also told that he still believes in "socialism," but certainly not in this Soviet socialism mounted on tank tracks. He has been very friendly with Sakharov, although not so much lately. He knows all those who lurk in the subterranean world of dissent, yet he offers them no point of reference; he is no leader, rather a loner. (His books have been translated abroad, his brother lives in exile in London.) Like everyone else in Moscow, both dissidents and conservatives, Roy Medvedev is waiting: for prosperity, for reforms, for the good life to come; for the post office to deliver his parcels to him, for the authorities to give him back possession of his apartment in the center of Moscow, which they refuse to do; for the secret police to arrest or not arrest him. The history of the USSR is like a long queue of people waiting for something. And they wait.

We sit together in Medvedev's minuscule study, its walls lined with bursting bookshelves that hang over us. There is nothing "sly" in our conversation. To be sure, the Western reporter interviewing him may wonder whether he isn't violating his journalistic privilege and immunity, which could come to an abrupt end, at worst with a one-way ticket home. But contact with the foreign correspondent is the drug the dissidents cannot do without, the palliative they need more desperately whenever the political climate turns ugly, before ultimately it overwhelms them. Yet, too much journalism can land them in Siberia.

140

VZ Roy Aleksandrovic, are you afraid?

RM No one can feel secure in a climate of repression. For some time now I have had no more telephone calls from my brother, who lives in London. The parcels he sends me, with books, clothes, and other things, are confiscated by the customs. For the past several days, that black car with two men sitting in it has been parked in front of my building. I don't know if they're going to nab me, we dissidents are always the last to find these things out. I've been told that someone in the Party's Central Committee wants me gagged, but the competent authorities haven't yet come to a decision.

VZ What are you afraid of, exactly?

RM Nothing. I don't think I'm afraid. I'm prepared. Arrest and deportation are distinctly possible in my case, all the same I'm calm and at peace. When I saw that the government was cracking down again with a certain regularity—someone arrested every week or ten days—I warned my family to be prepared for the worst. And here I am, waiting. I hope (he smiles faintly, but is it really a smile?) that the *Corriere della Sera* will give out the news if they should arrest me.

VZ You say you're not afraid. But the government is afraid. Why do they fear a few dozen dissidents so much?

RM Why was your great, powerful Roman Catholic Church so frightened of heretics and deviants that it even doomed them to be burned alive? From morning to night, with every conceivable means at its disposal, the Soviet government hammers in the notion that the people are united and compact, politically and morally, that there are no enemies of socialism or opponents of that . . . (he hesitates for a moment) . . . form of socialism that rules us. To accept the reality of even a handful of dissidents, to let them speak out, would mean confessing that our unity is imperfect, that the myth of solidarity between people and Party is false, and that all other derivative myths are also false.

VZ But still, the dissidents do speak out, although very little . . . for a month, a year . . .

141

RM   At first, the authorities deny that dissent exists; they look astonished if you ask them about it. Then they try to portray every dissident as a criminal who's been left unmolested only by the clemency of the government. And then, if the culprit refuses to repent, they arrest him and deport or expel him. But they must brand him as a criminal because no dialogue or discussion is possible. You must understand that describing Sakharov and other dissenters as criminals and spies is not an *a posteriori* cover-up but rather the government's way of thinking and acting. The government will not and cannot admit that political opposition exists in any form whatever.

VZ   Then why hasn't it silenced Sakharov once and for all, as Stalin would have done?

RM   Because this, too, is part of the government's behavioral scheme. Stalin was a tyrant, a fact which is almost officially confirmed. Today the authorities must show that they're different, therefore they make a show of flexibility. And they've devised a step-by-step system of retribution. Sakharov is so well known that the powers-that-be must proceed against him by stages. Instead of sending him to prison and then putting him on trial, which would provoke violent reactions throughout the world, they issue an administrative order committing him to exile in Gorky, a respectable city and not very far away. Thus, they eliminate any need for indictments, for proceedings or trials.

VZ   And after Gorky?

RM   Well, if he refuses to learn his lesson, they'll punish him more severely by exiling him to another city farther away, where things will go worse for him, and so on. Meanwhile, the government, which knows you Westerners better than you think, will distract your attention to weaken your negative reaction little by little. Moreover, the other dissidents, who thought Sakharov was untouchable, will likewise have plenty of time to mull over their own lesson. From Gorky Sakharov could be sent to Irkutsk in Siberia, to Tomsk, or to Chita. Worse every time. The mechanism is so simple, so efficient . . . how come you don't understand it? The important thing is that the victim must always have something to lose, therefore something to be afraid of.

VZ And that in defiance of world public opinion, of the doves, of Soviet friends and activists . . .

RM Of course the government realizes that it must pay a price. But détente was already pretty much ruined with the invasion of Afghanistan, and the international situation was extremely tense. What further damage could be caused by the arrest of Sakharov? You're all worried about Sakharov, as you should be, but not many of you have spoken out against the arrest of Father Dudko, the true leader of religious dissent, an author and intellectual, or Yakunin, his colleague, or Velikanova, who fought against many hardships to carry forward her clandestine *Chronicle of Current Events*. And there will be other arrests—of writers like Aksionov and Vladimov. Or of another thirty or forty dissidents, however many there are. Sanctions? A Soviet proverb says that even seven punishments are no worse than one, the first punishment. And really, Carter, who seems to dream up some new reprisal every morning, makes us laugh. But again, the point is something else. As I said before, dissent must be suppressed at all costs, and the will, the need, to liquidate it is stronger in the government than any fear of hurting our international relations. Where diplomatic opportunism is concerned, the government can wait—although not too long. And then when the moment comes, it will revert to repression. But look here . . . weren't there arrests and trials even during the best years of détente? Or does only Sakharov matter to you?

(The telephone rings incessantly. Sometimes it's a friend calling, or Medvedev's wife to ask if everything is all right. Sometimes it's no one ["Hello. Hello." No reply. Medvedev slams down the receiver], as often happens in Moscow: phone calls out of the void. When the police took Sakharov away, Roy Medvedev's line went dead for the whole day. Signals. Warnings. Watch out; you're only one step away from the abyss.)

VZ Roy Aleksandrovic, why does the Academy of Sciences refuse to

143

expel Sakharov when the government accuses him of "treachery," "espionage," and "moral unworthiness"?

RM Two-thirds of the Academy members must vote for his expulsion in a secret ballot; as yet there is no such majority. But not out of sympathy for Sakharov or opposition to the government . . . let's not deceive ourselves . . . but rather to avoid establishing a precedent that could endanger their own position as academicians. Since Stalin's death, no academician has been expelled, even though some of them have been charged with common crimes, corruption, and swindling. Other lesser cultural institutions have expelled members or sent them into early retirement, but no one has been thrown out of the Academy.

VZ But surely some eager academician or other must have asked for Sakharov's expulsion if only to ingratiate himself with the Party.

RM Of course. But to help you understand the situation, let me tell you a remarkable anecdote, really a striking coincidence. About twelve years ago, Sakharov himself asked the president of the Academy—it was Keldish then—to expel Trofim Lysenko, the notorious "biologist" and Stalin's favorite, who had wrecked the entire science of biology in the USSR and covered himself with infamy. He had instigated and led the fight to expel many of his enemies from the Academy, like Vavilov and others. And do you know what Keldish's answer was? You're right, Academician Sakharov, Lysenko deserves to be kicked out of the Academy. No one respects him, no one speaks to him any more, he's abandoned and despised, like a mangy dog. We all agree, Andrei Dimitric. But what would happen if one day someone asked me to expel *you?* Could I refuse after the Lysenko case has set a precedent?

It's an incredible paradox, don't you think?—the dissident Sakharov saved in his rank as an academician of the USSR by the shadow of the Stalinist Lysenko!

VZ At any rate, isn't it possible that there might be disagreements or some reluctance at the summit? I mean that someone might disapprove of the actions taken on Afghanistan, Sakharov, and other issues—perhaps Brezhnev himself?

144

RM Brezhnev works only two or three hours a day; he seems to be quite secure. Given this fact and the international crisis, probably a restricted group has formed, as on past occasions, to confront the emergency. This group, working twenty-four hours a day, would be represented by the bureaucracy, the major decision-making centers, the KGB, the Army, the diplomatic corps, the Party, and other elements. It would make its decisions in conformity with Brezhnev's wishes, certainly not against them. That isn't the Politburo's way of doing things, not as long as Brezhnev is alive and active.

VZ Apropos of international crises, Medvedev, what do you think of the Olympic boycott?

RM A mistake, a serious mistake, and I'll tell you why. Again you Westerners, especially Americans, are tripped up by your social and political convictions. Here, political decisions in no way depend upon public opinion, upon any pressures—what pressures?— or the mood of the people. The grain embargo won't deprive our leaders of a single glass of milk, a roll of bread, or a beefsteak. If anyone, it will be the people who suffer from the scarcity of food, and the poorer they are, the more they'll suffer. If the Olympics are canceled, it won't be the Central Committee that suffers but the athletes and the sports fans. What's more, since the government's propaganda machine is so powerful, indeed it's omnipresent, the government will seize this excellent opportunity to stir up a wave of anti-Americanism by stamping Carter and those in his camp as evil men, who snatch milk away from babies and medals from athletes, who are trying to force Russia to her knees and humiliate her in the eyes of the world. Do you really think that if we go without bread, Soviet citizens will march in protest on Red Square?

VZ Well, if Carter is naïve isn't the Italian Communist Party also naïve, wondering why the Kremlin can't confront dissent "politically"?

RM . . . The USSR isn't Italy or France, because the Soviet regime isn't founded on a majority or a total consensus, but on ideology.

145

Only Marxists, whatever that may mean today, have the right to rule; conversely, the ruling class justifies itself only by reference to the country's ideological foundations. It's a vicious circle, a religion, if you like. The USSR is the last great religious state on earth. Therefore, as I said before, every dissident, every heretic must be flushed out and gagged. This isn't a problem of quantity but of basic principles on which the regime rests. It's inconceivable that the regime would accept its own demise. . . .

I'm convinced however that socialism and pluralism can coexist, and I think you will find such a possibility mentioned in the works of Marx, Kautsky, and Lenin. Stalinism, to the contrary, introduced the concept of one-party totalitarianism as wholly arbitrary dogma; as I see it, such Stalinist concepts contradict the fundamental theories of Marxism-Leninism. In other words, to judge by Soviet thinking today, the central dogma of Marxism-Leninism is basically anti-Marxist and anti-Leninist. That's my view.

VZ   But in reality, where have you ever seen a pluralistic communism?

RM   In some countries, like Hungary and Czechoslovakia, conditions are already better than they are in the USSR. The Czech experiment was an effort to create a pluralistic society within socialism, but it failed because the Warsaw Pact countries intervened. . . . All the same, I'm still convinced that with time, socialism will assume that famous human face, and that pluralism will become one of the principles of the Soviet state.

VZ   You really are convinced of that?

RM   In theory, yes. Unfortunately, it's only a theory. In practice, no such socialism exists.

VZ   But what about the future, Roy Aleksandrovic? What will become of the dissident movement, of the hope for that human face, which no one has ever seen?

RM   I'm afraid that the future of the movement in the USSR is black. Very black. Here we have only a few dozen dissidents left; today there are more of them in Paris and New York than there are in Moscow. The leaders are now all in prison, in internal exile, or abroad. . . . The outlook is very dark indeed.

146

VZ Is there any one who could step into Sakharov's shoes?

RM No one, because no one has Sakharov's special qualities. No one could be a dissident, and at the same time part of the Soviet establishment, as he was. He was inside the sanctuary, not outside it or on the periphery. Imagine this: the last-but-one edition of the Great Soviet Encyclopedia, which came out when he was already a notorious dissident, published a long, exultant piece on him.

VZ So the curtain has fallen, and the KGB has finally won, is that it?

RM No, just the opposite. The bitter lessons of these past years, of these times, will be learned and deeply meditated on. A certain style of dissent is dying, no doubt about it. That dissent has achieved as much as it could, call it flights forward or individualism or whatever you like, but it's now in decline, it's going, it's moribund. With Sakharov in exile, a chapter has ended. But I hope, in fact I know, that a new generation is working, preparing—I mention no names—in Leningrad, for example, to pick up the ball where the old-timers have dropped it, and carry it forward into the '80s, perhaps beyond into the '90s, to 2000. They're young people, students, who have looked on and come to know the tremendous hardships dissent entails: the financial difficulties, the discouragements, the physical suffering, isolation, fear. They're trying to forge hooks for themselves and alliances to avoid being cut down every time they show their faces out of doors. They're trying to work with greater profundity.

VZ What do the Soviet people know about you, Roy Medvedev? What do you mean to them? Why should they take risks? Let sleeping dogs lie, they tell you.

RM Yes, I know. The petition in behalf of Sakharov was signed by barely twenty persons, all of them with one foot already in the courtroom. For the trials of the '60s there were thousands of signatures, hundreds for Siniavsky, Daniel, Ginzburg, and Galanksov. But dissent won't die; it's closing down and becoming transformed. This is imperative, otherwise no democratic development or reforms would be possible; to the contrary, repression would only worsen. The USSR needs dissent. It must exist, and I hope it does.

147

Index

Maltsev, Yuri, 116
Mandelstam, Osip, 20, 55, 82
Maoism, 88
Mao Zedong, 89-90
Marx, Karl, 66, 85, 87, 92, 97, 100, 112, 146; on censors, 3; and Engels: *The German Ideology*, 88; *Capital*, 89; *Communist Manifesto*, 90; *Theses on Feuerbach*, 90; saw his theory as philosophy of action, 90-91
Marxism, 42, 81, 99; socialism distinct from, 77-94
Marxism-Leninism, 66, 146; term, 87, 89, 90
Marxist (term), 87
Marxists, 146
Marxist theory, 65-66, 79-81, 90; guarantees freedom of opinion, 107
Marxist utopia, 90
Masses, 88
Mass media: Soviet, 8; Western, 118; *see also* Press
Master and Margarita (Bulgakov), 21n
Medvedev, Roy, 6-7; expulsion of, from CPSU, 25-36; attacks against, 130; harassment of, 139-47
Medvedev, Zhores, 7n, 16-17, 140; "Biological Science and the Personality Cult," 55; *Ten Years After Ivan Denisovich*, 60
Mendeleev, Dmitri, 109
Mensheviks, 92
Metropol (anthology), 135n, 136
Mikoyan, A. I., 18
Mill, John Stuart, 136-37
Ministry of the Interior, 96
Modernization, 49, 111
Moldavia, 48
Molotov, Vyacheslav, 18, 30
Monet, Claude, 21
Moroz, Valentyn, 45, 117n
Moscow, 8, 48, 117; city committee of CPSU, 26-27, 28-29
Murashov, Sergei I., 31, 32

NEP, *see* New Economic Policy
Nadezhda, Olitskaya, 55
Narodiniks, 133n
Nationalism (USSR), 74-76, 109, 124, 125
Nekrich, Aleksandr, 31
Neo-Stalinism, 53-66
New Economic Policy, 79, 80, 92
Newton, Isaac, 87
Nicholas I, tsar of Russia, 5n
Nikolaev, I., 25
Nixon, Richard M., 68
Nobel Peace Prize, 71, 86
Northern Caucasus, 50
Not by Bread Alone (Dudintsev), 58
Novocherkassk, 3
Novotny, Antonin, 73
Novy Mir, 25, 60, 61, 67, 83, 127

Oak and the Calf, The (Solzhenitsyn), 61
Obninsk, 6
October revolution, 48, 74, 75, 108, 109
Old Bolsheviks, 7, 18, 25, 26, 29
Olympic boycott (proposed), 145
One Day in the Life of Ivan Denisovich, 8, 32, 58, 59, 60, 127-28
On Socialist Democracy (R. Medvedev), 17
Opposition, as insanity, 102
Organizations, opposition, 116, 119-21; objections to, 120-22
Orlov, Yuri, 68, 116, 130
Outcasts (Sokolov), 137

Panin, Dmitry, 125
Pasternak, Boris, 20
Paustovsky, Konstantin, 127
Pavlov, Ivan P., 109
"Peasant literature," 63
Peasants, 96, 101; in China, 91
Pelshe, Arvid, 32
Penal code, 45, 85-86; *Article 70*, 24, 44; *Article 74*, 45; *Article 190*, 24, 27n